Workbook for *Telling the Story*

The Convergence of Print, Broadcast and Online Media

FIFTH EDITION

Workbook for Telling the Story

The Convergence of Print, Broadcast and Online Media

THE MISSOURI GROUP

Brian S. Brooks

George Kennedy

Daryl R. Moen

Don Ranly

School of Journalism
University of Missouri–Columbia

Bedford/St. Martin's
Boston • New York

For Bedford/St. Martin's

Publisher for Communication: Erika Gutierrez
Senior Editor: Karen Schultz Moore
Developmental Editor: Linda Stern
Editorial Assistant: Caitlin Crandell
Production Assistant: Laura Winstead
Senior Production Supervisor: Dennis J. Conroy
Marketing Manager: Stacey Propps
Project Management: Books By Design, Inc.
Cover Design: Billy Boardman
Composition: Books By Design, Inc.
Printing and Binding: Malloy Lithographing, Inc.

President, Bedford/St. Martin's: Denise B. Wydra
Presidents, Macmillan Higher Education: Joan E. Feinberg and Tom Scotty
Director of Development: Erica T. Appel
Director of Marketing: Karen R. Soeltz
Production Director: Susan W. Brown
Associate Production Director: Elise S. Kaiser
Manager, Publishing Services: Andrea Cava

Manufactured in the United States of America.

7 6
f e d c b

For information, write: Bedford/St. Martin's, 75 Arlington Street, Boston, MA 02116
   (617-399-4000)

ISBN 978-1-4576-1926-7

Acknowledgments
Acknowledgments and copyrights are continued at the back of the book on page 135, which constitutes an extension of the copyright page.

Preface

The *Workbook for Telling the Story*, Fifth Edition, has been reorganized and revised to match the new edition of the text. It has also been updated to provide a strong focus on the challenges that you, as a journalist, will face in the converging newsrooms of the 21st century. We have achieved this focus by maintaining our emphasis on the basics of reporting and writing, even as we included coverage of digital media, including social media.

While the text provides explanations that help you understand and develop the attitudes and skills required by the multimedia work environment, this workbook presents thought-provoking exercises that enable you to practice those skills.

You'll discover that the *Workbook for Telling the Story* is thoroughly practical. Its exercises are tied directly and clearly to the principles explained in the text. The exercises provide more variety and allow for more practice, especially with the computer as a learning tool. Perhaps the most valuable experience these exercises offer is participation in the discussions that will inevitably follow.

Each chapter features at least one Challenge Exercise; these ask you to test your skills on a more advanced level. There is also an added focus on technology and writing for multiple media. Finally, we have included a fictional city directory that allows you to conveniently hone your investigative skills as you work through the exercises. You should determine when to use the directory in checking facts and investigating stories.

We have included many more exercises than one term can accommodate. Your instructor may assign only select exercises. But you may want to do other exercises on your own for extra practice. The resources for both approaches are here. So, of course, is the option of altering or adding to any of these exercises to fit local conditions or to include local examples.

The principles and exercises offered in the text and in this workbook are well-tested. We use them in our own teaching. Hundreds of other instructors in courses throughout the United States (and beyond) have done the same. To all those colleagues who have offered suggestions and examples, we extend thanks.

We appreciate the work done by the staff at Bedford/St. Martin's, especially by publisher Erika Gutierrez, senior editor Karen Schultz Moore, developmental editor Linda Stern, editorial assistant Caitlin Crandell, and senior production supervisor Dennis Conroy.

Brian S. Brooks
George Kennedy
Daryl R. Moen
Dan Ranly

Contents

The Nature of News

1. Let's see what the news of the day is around the world. A good place to start is the popular website Google News (http://news.google.com), which brings together headlines from multiple news sources. There you'll find the most recent stories from news organizations around the world. Open and read three or four news items from non-American sources. In a one-page report, explain how they differ in style and content from the stories you see every day in the American media.

2. Newsy.com compiles video news stories from a wide variety of sources. Take a look at one day's reports, and see what you can discover about the different perspectives provided by those sources.

3. As a team exercise, work with two or three classmates to examine the news of the day in your local media. Each team member will prepare a short report, and then the group will compare them. How do news judgments vary? How does each source fulfill the functions of journalism described in Chapter 1?

4. Chapter 1 offers a definition of journalistic bias that is probably different from any you have read elsewhere. How well does this definition match what you see in the news?

5. Go to Journalism.org, and take a look at the latest *State of the News Media* report. Pick one section of the report, and write a news story on its content.

6. Check out online news sites such as CNN.com, NYTimes.com, and your local newspaper's home page. Then write a short paragraph or blog post addressing the following questions.
   a. Compare the content of the newspapers and television news available in your community with what's available online. What do you find in one source that's unavailable in others?
   b. Which best satisfies your appetite for news?
   c. Which do you find most enjoyable to use?

7. Get copies of one day's newspapers from your city and at least one nearby city, plus a copy of *USA Today*. Write a one-page report comparing the local papers with *USA Today*.
   a. Analyze the news decisions of the editors by applying the criteria discussed in Chapter 1.
   b. As a national paper, *USA Today* has no local audience. How does that fact affect its editors' news decisions? How do the editors attempt to meet "local" interests across the nation?

8. Spend some time browsing the websites of America's two leading journalism reviews: the *Columbia Journalism Review* (www.cjr.org) and the *American Journalism Review* (www.ajr.org). Which do you find most relevant, useful and interesting? Why?

9. A. Review the elements of a good story in your textbook. Then in one or two sentences, explain what element or elements of each of the following events make it newsworthy.
   a. Police Chief Carlos Briceno is named Man of the Year by the local chamber of commerce.
   b. A store employee who reported a fire that did extensive damage to the store last night was taken into custody after police discovered that the store had been burglarized and found some of the merchandise in the employee's car.
   c. A national study found that the local cancer detection center has the highest rate of inaccurate diagnoses in the nation. The director of the center disputes the findings.

   B. Imagine that you are the news editor of your local newspaper. Rank the preceding three events in order of their news value. Justify your decisions to the managing editor, your boss.

10. a. Imagine that your school has just announced that conservative spokesperson Patrick Buchanan and the national American Civil Liberties Union president will debate drug testing next week on campus. Your assignment as a reporter is to prepare a background story on the issue. Go to the library and find six sources of information. List them and note which, if either, side of the issue each source is likely to reflect.
    b. Now describe how you will find and evaluate *local* sources for the same story.

11. a. Your assignment as a reporter is to do a story on one of the following: religious conflict in the Middle East, capital punishment, the use of animals in laboratory experiments, air traffic safety. Use the library to find as many sources as you'll need for a story that will be fair and complete. Identify your sources and their likely viewpoints.
    b. Describe how you will find local sources for that story. How might you evaluate the qualifications of such sources?

12. Imagine that you are a reporter pursuing a story about the death of a child after an apparently simple operation at a local hospital. You establish that the incident happened, and you confirm enough details for a story. You are unable to learn the name of the surgeon who performed the operation, but you do learn the name of the nurse who was responsible for

postoperative care and who was on duty when the child died. You also learn that the nurse was transferred to another job immediately after the death. However, no one will say whether the transfer was related to the incident.

Would it be fair to publish the name of the nurse? In one or two paragraphs, state and explain your response.

13. At the *Columbia Missourian*, an accuracy-checking policy requires that the facts in every story be double-checked with the sources who provided them before the story is published. Few newspapers follow such a policy. On many papers, editors do not allow sources to see stories or to have stories read to them before publication, for fear of improper influence on the way the stories are handled.

List the advantages and possible disadvantages of accurately checking stories before publication by showing or reading them to the people who provided the information. Be prepared to discuss your ideas in class.

14. Do an accuracy check on your local newspaper. Choose five local stories, make copies of them and send them to everybody you can identify as either a source of information or a subject of the story. Your instructor will help you draft a letter that explains your purpose. Ask whether the details and the overall tone of the story are correct. Ask the respondents for specific praise or criticism. If you undertake this as a class project, you may get an idea of how fair and accurate your local newspaper's coverage is.

15. CHALLENGE EXERCISE
Figure 1.1 in the text illustrates the differences in accuracy, fairness and bias between news stories and commentaries. Read a week's worth of your local newspaper's coverage of a major issue. Then look at the opinion pages to see how editorials deal with that issue. What differences in tone and substance do you find? Write a short report explaining your findings.

2 Convergence, Citizen Journalism and Emerging Media

1. Go to the websites of two national news sources (such as CNN and *The New York Times*). Find examples of citizen-produced journalism on those sites, and describe how that content fits with the rest of the site's content. Does it complement it or conflict with it? Does citizen-produced content seem popular with consumers?

2. Examine the content of one online news source. Compare the online source's national and international coverage of today's events with coverage of the same events on one of tonight's national news broadcasts and in tomorrow's edition of your local newspaper. Describe your findings in a two-page report.

3. Find the online version of a local newspaper. Write a two-page report comparing the content of that newspaper with that of your college or university newspaper. Did the two papers cover any of the same stories? Is the emphasis in coverage different? If so, how does that emphasis speak to the needs of the two papers' audiences?

4. Examine the online version of a local daily newspaper to identify any sections that ask for reader input or that are updated in the style of a blog. After reviewing two or three articles that ask for feedback, post a comment on the newspaper's discussion board or blog. How does this change the relationship between journalist and reader? Be prepared to discuss your thoughts.

5. List two or three sources in which you might find information on the number of newspapers owned by major newspaper companies in the U.S. Using one of them, list the number of newspapers owned by Gannett Co., the nation's largest newspaper company. What is Gannett's flagship newspaper?

6. Using online databases or the Internet, list at least five media operations owned by The Walt Disney Co.

7. Visit Newsy.com, which attempts to provide a more balanced approach to the news by showing multiple views of how a story is covered, and view three stories. Write a one-page assessment of how well the site fulfills its purpose. How could it be better?

8. Find someone who started his or her own website (or a fan page on Facebook or a similar social media site). Does the site attempt to make a profit and therefore support its founder? If it does, discuss with the founder the skills needed to make the site successful. If profit is not a goal, ask how the site owner plans to keep the site going with little or no income. Summarize your results in a brief report.

9. Find an example of a hyperlocal news site published by a major newspaper or television station. Analyze its content, and describe how it differs from the content of the parent publication.

10. Arrange a visit to a local newspaper or broadcast station, or your campus newspaper or radio station. Produce a chart that shows the organizational structure of the operation.

11. News delivery over mobile phones is increasingly popular. Find three media outlets in your area that distribute news in this way. Which one does the best job? Why?

12. **CHALLENGE EXERCISE**
Talk with a reporter from your local newspaper or broadcast station about finding a first job in the industry. Based on your discussion, list the steps you would take to find your first job.

3 Interviewing

1. As you've seen in Chapter 3 of the text, the key to a good interview is establishing rapport with your source. You've been assigned to do a profile of a new instructor on campus. You don't know this person at all. How will you try to establish rapport?

2. The best interviews are often described as conversations. Of course, as with many of the guidelines in journalism, that isn't always the case. When might the "interview as conversation" model not be the best approach?

3. Often the best interviews are determined by the amount of preparation the reporter does before the interview. One way is to prepare a memo for yourself. Write a memo of up to two pages to prepare for each of the following interviews. You can use a database for research, but you don't need to restrict yourself to database sources. Indicate the sources of your information.
   a. Your state's governor. Concentrate on details that will allow you to focus on the governor's stand on higher education.
   b. Your state's junior U.S. senator. Concentrate on details that will allow you to focus on his or her stand on gun control.
   c. Your congressional representative. Concentrate on details that will allow you to focus on his or her stand on abortion.
   d. The vice president of the U.S. Concentrate on details that will allow you to focus on the vice president's stand on aid to higher education.
   e. Jon Stewart. The comedian is also a skilled interviewer. Concentrate on how he prepares for interviews.
   f. Sarah Palin. As a politician and television personality, she has a well-known aversion to mainstream journalists. Concentrate on how you might try to overcome that.
   g. The chief executive officer of your campus. Concentrate on details that will allow you to focus on his or her view of the role of fraternities and sororities on campus.
   h. The dean or chair of your journalism school or department. Concentrate on details that will allow you to focus on the role of professional experience in the training of an educator.
   i. The director of the local chamber of commerce. Concentrate on details that will allow you to focus on his or her views on promoting retail business.

4. Conduct an interview with your instructor, who will play the part of one of the people in Exercise 3. Write a 500-word story.

5. This exercise requires a video camera or a cellphone with video capability. Team up with a classmate, and interview each other on camera. Edit each interview to one and a half minutes. Share the interviews online with the class, and critique them.

6. You've seen athletes interviewed on television. (If not, spend some time watching ESPN.) Track down an athlete on campus, and interview her or him. Write a story. Then check its accuracy with the subject. How did you do?

7. Find someone to interview at a local senior citizen center. Focus on the person's attitude toward news. Where does this person get news, and what does he or she think of journalism today? Write a story, and check its accuracy.

8. Journalists must establish rapport quickly with sources.
   a. Watch one of the network or cable morning news shows. Evaluate the rapport, or lack of it, between the interviewer and a source. Present evidence to support your assessment.

   b. How would you establish rapport with the source interviewed on the news show? List specific steps you would take.

9. With two classmates, pick a topic for an interview. Each of you will interview a different person. One will conduct the interview in person, one by telephone or Skype, and one by email. Compare notes and impressions. Which method was most successful?

10. Select a story from your campus or local newspaper about a local source. (Do not choose a report of a meeting.) Send or take it to the main source, and ask the source to identify errors of fact or context. Find out whether the interview was conducted by phone or in person. If the interview was conducted in person, find out where it occurred and how long it lasted. Critique the work of the reporter.

11. Interview a journalist from a local news organization. Ask the journalist to describe his or her most successful and least successful efforts at establishing rapport. Write a report.

12. Your instructor will ask the class to listen to a prepared statement. Take notes. No questions will be permitted. Now reproduce the statement as best you can. Compare your version against the original. Is it accurate down to the articles and conjunctions?

13. Your instructor will invite someone to appear before the class to make a statement and to answer a few questions. The session will be recorded. Write a story based on the interview. Then check the accuracy of your story against the recording.

14. Using a database, find the original text of a presidential speech or news conference. Then find two versions of the story published in newspapers, in either their print or online editions. For instance, compare stories done by *The New York Times* and the Associated Press. Check the accuracy of the quotes in the stories against the transcript. Describe and evaluate any discrepancies.

15. Imagine your editor calls you into the office to tell you that a source in your story claims he was misquoted. You show the editor the quote in your notebook. How will the editor know whether you or the source is right? How will you know?

16. The results of a national study on the average costs of college education show the following figures from the 2008–2009 school year:

	Men	Women	White	Black	Hispanic
Tuition/fees	$6,045	$4,830	$4,969	$4,821	$4,108
Books/supplies	$821	$807	$811	$831	$674
Room/board	$6,431	$6,533	$6,518	$6,121	$4,613

You have been assigned to do a story based on the national study but with a local focus.

a. Whom would you interview at your local college?

b. What further information would you want in hand before conducting any interviews?

c. Prepare a list of questions for one of your key sources.

17. CHALLENGE EXERCISE

Last week, after an eight-year tenure, Barbara Behling resigned as chancellor of Springfield University. Behling took office at a time of waning state support. Her decisions on funding priorities and efforts to upgrade the physical appearance and integrity of the campus generated controversy. Below is the interview you conducted with Behling.

a. Write a 500-word story based on this interview.

b. List some of the follow-up questions you would like to ask based on the answers Behling gave.

Q: Think back. What was the university like when you came here? What were your primary challenges?

A: I wasn't really ready to leave Oklahoma, but a friend of mine had told me that this was a challenge that would interest me. What really intrigued me was the attitude of the search committee. It clearly portrayed an institution that was ready for some change.

The four earliest problem areas were the hospital, the physical plant, administrative structuring and minority recruitment.

The hospital was a big one. It was not in good financial shape. Bills were being delayed and not aggressively collected. The legislature was concerned about hospital financing. The place looked bad. There was no stopping and thinking about whether I had to do something; it had to be done.

Q: What did you do?

A: The first thing I did was hire a consultant to find out what was wrong with the operation. I learned a lot about hospital administration in a hurry. We made some personnel changes and recruited the current director, who came in with a lot of experience and put a plan together.

That first-year budget was about $50 million, with about a third of that coming from the state. Today, the budget is about $125 million, with only about 15 percent coming from the state. Remember, the hospital is there to serve the medical school. It's unique because it is a teaching hospital, but at the same time, it has to pay its bills. We constantly ask ourselves which is the tail and which is the dog.

Q: How about the physical renovation?

A: One of the first proposals made to me was for an addition to the law school building. I asked questions like, "Do you need the space? Show me the documentation. Is other space on campus available? Is this the best solution?"

The point is, it made me realize how much work there was to do in the area of physical planning.

I divided the job into three parts. One was to hire a consultant to give me a list of highly visible projects that could be done at reasonable cost and would make a quick impression of progress to make the campus look better and make people feel better about it. Renovation of the south grounds of Jesse Hall and Jesse Auditorium were on that list.

The second part was to get good documentation on upkeep of the buildings, maintenance schedules and the like.

Third was to begin major planning for the campus. This plan is being used to guide about $145 million worth of construction that has been completed or is in process at a time when funds have been extremely scarce.

Q: Let's turn now to minority recruitment. Is part of the problem that there just aren't enough minority college students to go around?

A: Of the college-age minorities living in this state, we don't get our share applying to our school. This is a national problem. The population is becoming increasingly minority. It is the segment of the population that participates in higher education the least, and we will become increasingly dependent on them in the future to help run the society.

Q: Once all roadblocks are down and minorities are clearly encouraged to enroll, what else can you do?

A: Soon after I came here and had done a lot of inquiry into this, I used to say I did not know of anyone on campus who would willingly admit they were against minority participation, but they didn't make it a priority. We must continue to make it a priority.

Q: Is it a priority on this campus now?

A: It is in many areas—at least in some. Giving equal treatment is not enough. We need to do unusual things to recruit and keep minorities.

Q: Does this mean we need to practice affirmative action?

A: For years, minorities have had disadvantaged backgrounds. We have to give them extraordinary opportunities to succeed.

Q: Can you be more specific?

A: We are making a special effort to recruit minority faculty, to have minority speakers on campus, to recruit high school minority students, to give enough scholarship aid for minorities and to provide special academic support in the form of teaching study skills in math and writing.

Q: What was the problem you identified in the structure of the central administration?

A: I immediately found a problem with centralization in research administration. Too many approvals were required. There were too many stumbling blocks from the large structure at the central administration. I had a research position to be filled (graduate dean for research), so through that, I actually began to understand the university.

As is true on all campuses, as the student body had grown through the years, the administration had grown. It's very easy to put new people in without rethinking the total organization. As I recall, at the time I came, there were some 26 people reporting directly to the chancellor. There was considerable ambiguity about where decisions finally were made. I personally like to function with a smaller staff having broader responsibilities.

I had a lot to learn in a short time about the institution. I had to do a lot of listening. The basic thing I did was to think through what the campus is for. It's there to serve students academically, so I decided to reduce from three provosts to one provost for academics.

Gathering and Verifying Information

4

1. You are writing a story about U.S. immigration policies and their impact on the workforce. Find the address and phone number of the closest office of the U.S. Bureau of Citizenship and Immigration Services, which would be a primary source of information for such a story. List at least five other possible sources.

2. You are writing a story about nanotechnology and its promise in medicine. What might be a primary source of information for such a story? List at least five other possible sources.

3. Your instructor will give you the names of 10 local people. Using reference materials available in your library and online, determine the occupation of each.

4. Using online reference materials, write a half-page biographical sketch of each of the following people, as if you were preparing a story for an impending visit of that person to your campus:
   a. Hilda Solis
   b. Spike Lee
   c. Carrie Underwood

    d. Will Ferrell

    e. Camilla Parker Bowles

    f. Garth Brooks

    g. Ruth Bader Ginsburg

    h. Nancy Pelosi

    i. Bill Richardson

    j. Howard Stern

    k. Henry Aaron

    l. Se Ri Pak

    m. Chris Bosh

    n. Venus Williams

    o. Chris Hemsworth

5. Using reference materials available online or in your college or local library, answer the following questions:

    a. What was the final popular vote in the 2012 presidential election?

    b. What was the electoral vote in the same election?

6. Who are the U.S. senators from the following states?

    a. Florida

    b. Kansas

    c. Tennessee

    d. Missouri

    e. Washington

    f. California

    g. Illinois

    h. New York

    i. Maine

    j. North Carolina

7. Using any reference materials available to you, list the largest city in each of the following states:

    a. New Hampshire

    b. Connecticut

    c. Mississippi

    d. Utah

    e. Colorado

    f. Alabama

    g. Iowa

    h. Ohio

    i. Kentucky

    j. North Dakota

8. What are the primary cash crops of the following countries?

    a. India

    b. Germany

    c. Kenya

    d. Romania

    e. Canada

    f. Colombia

    g. Argentina

h. Egypt
i. Mongolia
j. New Zealand

9. Determine when your city was incorporated and what its population was in 1960, 1970, 1980, 1990, 2000 and 2010.

10. Without talking with your mayor or town supervisor, where would you find the following information about him or her?
    a. The official's address and telephone number
    b. The amount the official paid for his or her house
    c. The number of cars the official owns
    d. The names and ages of the official's children, if any
    e. What property, if any, the official owns, other than his or her primary residence

11. Using a financial database such as Yahoo Finance, determine the names of the principal officers of AOL and their salaries. List at least the five top officers.

12. Using any available database, determine the closing price of a share of stock in the following companies for each trading day during the past week:
    a. MarkWest Energy Partners
    b. Texas Instruments
    c. RJR Nabisco
    d. The Walt Disney Co.
    e. IBM

13. Using any online service, call up the major news story of the day from the Associated Press and any other wire service (such as Reuters), and compare the two. Tell which is the better story and why.

14. Which database would be most useful in helping you locate magazine articles on the decline of daily newspaper circulation? Why?

15. A local women's clothing boutique has just gone out of business. After interviewing the local managers of that store and the remaining stores in the area, you decide that your story needs background information about trends in retail marketing. Determine what traditional sources of

information you could use for background data or insight. Then outline a strategy you could use to conduct a database search of material related to the topic.

16. You receive a press release stating that a local McDonald's hamburger outlet is the second most profitable in a six-state region. Determine what traditional sources of information you could use for background data or insight. Then outline a strategy you could use to conduct a database search of material related to the topic.

17. Read the following story, and then make a list of the obvious sources the reporter used to develop the story. List at least three other sources that could have been used to improve the story.

Farming is at the top of the state's killer occupation list. And if anyone is going to knock it from the top, it will probably be a mom.

Bad prices and competition from an increasing number of larger producers have put the squeeze on farmers, who are forced to maximize their land, capital, labor and time. The pressure, in turn, eliminates time-consuming safety practices.

The Springfield University Extension Service has developed a three-year safety program that targets women, who are the best at starting safety practices on the farm and in the home, said David Baker, University Extension safety specialist.

Among dangerous occupations, farming ranks high, the result of long hours, neglected machinery, farm animals and a wide range of ages among farmers, Baker said. The job of safety guard is usually included in women's daily farm and housework challenges. Women teach values and attitudes to the next generation. They think more about safety and health because they deal with it every day, Baker said.

Women throughout the state, like Jan Hedeman, are doing farm work they may not have been trained to do.

They have become truck drivers, grain haulers, tractor drivers and machinery operators. They are also learning more efficient ways to protect their families from possible tragedies using these machines.

Hedeman is the president of the Dade County Extension Council. She and her husband, Terry, sponsored a Farm Women's Safety Seminar in February.

The seminar was the third in a series of one-day workshops scattered throughout the state in 11 counties from February to April. The seminars give the state's women hands-on experience with machinery and teach them how to prevent accidents. They also discuss various health issues.

Of 38 farm deaths in the state in 1990, 35 involved machinery, said Rusty Lee, an extension associate.

Twenty-eight farmers were killed on tractors, five on mowers, two on other machinery, two by electrocution and one while tree cutting.

At the workshop on the Hedemans' farm, two emergency medical technicians showed the women how to perform first aid and contact emergency services.

Hedeman said, "You always know safety is important, but it's hard to remember and practice all the time. These seminars are a good reminder.

"We own a mixture of tractors and other equipment, so the women were exposed to different brands and types of machinery. We learned bush hogs can be the most dangerous machines on the farm. We also went over tractor controls and PTO shafts."

Bush hogs are farming implements that hook onto the back of a tractor and are used to mow grasses. The tractor driver must be extremely careful. The spinning blade can spit out rocks like bullets and take out small trees easily.

The PTO, or power takeoff, is a shaft that rotates at about 540 revolutions per minute. When it is not properly guarded, a person's clothes may become entangled in the shaft in a fraction of a second.

"It's obvious women are concerned about farm safety," Lee said. "We have been welcomed with open arms in every county."

Support for the program is coming from women's groups, including the Farm Bureau, the Agricultural Machinery Dealers Association, county fire and rescue personnel, community nurses and the University Extension staff, Baker said.

The National Institute for Occupational Safety and Health will fund the three-year project at a cost of $350,000. The workshops are only one part of the program.

The next women's safety seminar is March 5 in Lawrence County. To learn more, contact David Baker or Rusty Lee of University Extension at 555-2731.

18. Read the following story, and then make a list of the obvious sources the reporter used to develop the story. List at least three other sources that could have been used to improve the story.

The closing of Eighth Street between Walnut and Ash streets is one step closer to reality, as are plans for a town square and county administration building.

Some Springfield City Council members wanted to wait for a traffic study before making a decision on the county's request to close the block, but the study would have delayed plans for up to four months.

Now City Manager Diane Lusby wants to bypass the study, which was the only thing delaying a decision on the street.

In a recommendation to the council tonight, Lusby will tell members that once a decision is made, the city staff will work around any problems that may develop.

Lack of information about the impact on downtown traffic patterns and the future location of a new downtown fire station were some of the concerns members voiced last Monday at a joint meeting between city council and county officials.

Lincoln County Commissioner Nicole Ziden said closing Eighth Street is essential to the design of the new administration building.

"What we do with Eighth Street will determine what type of building and its placement," she said. "It's a fundamental question to this project."

Also affected by the decision are plans for a town square, which Commissioner Andrew Kramer said Springfield does not have.

"With the courthouse addition nearly complete, now is the opportune time to address landscaping needs," he said.

"We may never have an opportunity like this again, or at least not for a long, long time," Kramer said.

Besides providing a public gathering place and a much-needed green space downtown, closing the block will provide a safer way for county employees to move between the courthouse and their new building.

Area businesspeople also support closing the block, thereby removing the hazardous intersection at Eighth and Walnut streets.

"I'm in that intersection daily, and I am amazed people don't get killed every day," said Jeanne Matten, who has an office in the Guitar Building.

The New York architectural firm of Les Dally, which was selected to design the administrative building, may be assisting local architects with designing the plaza, Ziden said.

Dally has experience with adding new government buildings to existing structures and planning green spaces. Dally was responsible for the veterans' memorial and state information center in the state capital.

Kramer said closing the block would not create much of a problem if the city considered changing some one-way streets to two-way streets again.

"It's one of the deals where you have to decide what you really want in the downtown area and then do it and make traffic work around it," he said.

Jose Rodriguez, assistant city manager, said the city is still reviewing sites for the new downtown fire station. He said the station will probably be located north of Broadway between Sixth Street and College Avenue.

19. Prepare a complete dossier on the life of movie director and producer Steven Spielberg as if you were about to interview him for a major story.

20. CHALLENGE EXERCISE
You have been assigned to write a business article on the endorsement income of golfer Tiger Woods. Using online database services and traditional sources, find all the information you can on his various endorsement deals.

5 Reporting with Numbers

1. A local college has released figures showing that its total budget is $120 million. Of that total, $80 million comes from the state, $6 million from student tuition and the remaining $34 million from fees, grants and gifts.
   a. Figure the percentage of the college's budget that comes from each source.
   b. Identify the significance of each funding source.
   c. Using plain words instead of numbers, explain the proportion of funding that comes from the different sources.

2. At a campaign rally for a Democratic candidate for Congress, Springfield Mayor Juanita Williams criticized the incumbent member of Congress, a Republican, for missing 53 roll-call votes last year.
   a. What facts about Williams and the Republican and Democratic candidates would you need to know to write a balanced story about roll-call votes? What sources would you need to contact?
   b. Visit http://clerk.house.gov to find out how many roll-call votes were held in the U.S. House of Representatives during the last congressional session. Calculate the percentage of votes the member of Congress from your district missed. How does that attendance record compare with that of other members of the congressional delegation from your state?

3. You are an education reporter. Area school committees have released their annual budget figures after the beginning of the school year. Here are some base figures:

	Students		Budget	
	2011	2012	2011	2012
Springfield	4,650	4,724	$23,250,000	$23,620,000
Newburg	2,325	2,362	$12,787,500	$12,991,000
Hampton	1,211	1,101	$4,450,425	$3,496,000
Middletown	1,004	1,213	$7,530,000	$7,530,000

   a. Figure the per capita spending in each school district in both budget years.
   b. Figure the percentage change in per capita spending in each school district.

4. Using the data from Exercise 3, identify the following trends in the four school districts:
   a. Figure the percentage change in the number of students from year to year.
   b. Figure the percentage change in budgets from year to year.

5. Again using the data from Exercise 3, identify some of the basic financial issues facing the different school districts. Outline additional information that would be needed to write a balanced story about school funding. Suggest probable sources.

6. A group of resident advisers in the dormitories at Springfield University has asked to meet with the editorial board of the campus paper about conditions on the job. They complain that many RAs have seen their adviser-to-resident ratio increase 100 percent since last year, though their pay rate has remained the same. In preparation for the meeting, you phone the university's Campus Living Office. The director tells you that some resident advisers have seen their workload double because several wings of single rooms have been converted to double rooms to lower costs for students living on campus. She also says that resident advisers in some dormitories have even higher workloads. The director has scheduled a meeting with the advisers for next week. The number of resident advisers affected is seven out of a total of 42. The seven resident advisers now serve 36 residents each, instead of 18 each. The total number of students living on campus is 1,357.
   a. To get ready for the editorial board meeting with the resident advisers, prepare the numerical figures necessary to ask appropriate questions. Outline additional financial information that would help you determine if the university and the resident advisers are being reasonable.
   b. Craft a tentative lead for the next day's paper using words, not percentage figures.

7. Your editor assigns you to do a story about prison sentences handed down in cases of aggravated assault. He gives you the following figures from an anti-crime group that is lobbying for tougher sentencing guidelines. The cases represent the people convicted for aggravated assault in Springfield during one month in 2012.

Name	Sentence
Donald Kimball	1 year in prison, 2 years' probation
Christian Pelletier	1 year in prison, 1 year's probation
Robert Mitchell	14 months in prison, 1 year's probation
Nancy Newberry	1 year in prison, 1 year's probation
Mitchell Smith	1 year in prison, 2 years' probation
Lyle Rothstein	8 months in prison, 1 year's probation
Michael Hamlet	7 years in prison, 5 years' probation

   a. Calculate the arithmetic mean (average) prison term for people convicted of aggravated assault, taking care to convert some of the terms to figures that will compare properly (months versus years).
   b. Calculate the median prison term for people convicted of aggravated assault.
   c. Decide whether the mean or the median is the more accurate description of prison terms, and explain why.

8. Local multimillionaire David Dankowski has announced that he will provide low-interest loans of $1,000 for local low-income teenagers who go to college. He will charge a simple interest rate of 3 percent per year.
   a. If a student accepts a $1,000 loan from Dankowski for just one year, how much will the student owe Dankowski after one year? After graduating in five years?
   b. If the student accepts a $1,000 loan for each of her five years in college, how much will the student owe after graduation?

9. Tom's Café, a local coffee shop that has been in business since 1990, has raised its price for coffee for the first time since its founding. The price had been 50 cents for a cup of coffee. The new price is $1 a cup.
   a. Calculate the percentage increase in the price of a cup of coffee.
   b. Adjust the old price for inflation in the last full calendar year. In real dollars, is Tom's Café charging more for a cup of coffee now than it was in 1990?

10. Mayor Juanita Williams says in a campaign speech that she is proud that starting teachers' salaries in Springfield have increased from an average of $22,000 per year in 2002 to $30,000 in 2012. Across town, Republican Jesse Abraham accuses Williams of coddling Springfield teachers with a 50 percent pay increase during her 10 years on the City Council in order to win votes.
   a. Using the Consumer Price Index available on the Web (see sites listed in your textbook), calculate how much the 2002 starting salary would be worth in 2012 dollars.
   b. Explain whether Williams' statement about starting salaries is accurate and fair.
   c. Explain whether the numbers behind Abraham's statement about Williams are accurate and fair.

11. Officials in your county are proposing a county sales tax of 1 percent on top of the state's 6 percent sales tax. The state tax collected from the county's businesses last year totaled $5.88 million. Salespeople in businesses from boutiques to auto dealerships claim that shoppers will avoid their stores and shop in another county if the tax is imposed. You want to test those claims by examining the difference in costs caused by the higher taxes.
   a. Calculate the dollar increase in the cost of a $25 shirt.
   b. Calculate the dollar increase in the cost of a $1,540 computer.
   c. Calculate the dollar increase in the cost of a $15,000 car.
   d. If sales match last year's, how much will the new 1 percent sales tax produce for the county?
   e. Examine the credibility of the claims that increased sales tax will drive away shoppers, and suggest possible sources to interview about the issue.

12. The state legislature is considering exempting restaurant food sales from the sales tax in the same way grocery food sales are exempt.
   a. Explain how much fast-food patrons would save per year if they spend $5 per meal once a week.

    b. Explain how much restaurant patrons would save per year if they spend $20 per meal once a week.

    c. Go to a listing of sales taxes by states (for example, the Sales Tax Clearinghouse at http://thestc.com/STrates.stm), and compare your state against the states with the highest and lowest sales taxes.

13. A local factory has filed papers with the city declaring that it is overvalued and should be assessed at a value of $80 million instead of the $136 million assessed by the city. The millage rate is 23.80. How much tax revenue would the city lose if the factory wins the decision?

14. Refer to the budget document known as General Fund—Summary (Figure 5.1) in the textbook to answer the following questions:

    a. Under Department Expenditures, which category of appropriations has shown the greatest percentage increase from Actual Fiscal Year 2010 to Actual Fiscal Year 2011? What is the percentage?

    b. In percentage terms, has the Police Department or the Fire Department received the bigger increase over the two years?

    c. Now go back up to Appropriations. Personnel services appropriations have increased from $9.5 million in 2010 to $12.2 million in the budget adopted for 2012. Is that an increase in personnel services' share of the total operating budget? Explain.

15. The city whose budget appears in Figure 5.1 has 84,500 residents. Find the total budget under Actual Fiscal Year 2011, and calculate the per capita expenditures. Do the same for the Adopted Fiscal Year 2012 budget.

16. Referring to the same General Fund summary, the city manager issued this brief statement:

> Your city ended the last fiscal year in excellent financial health. We were able to increase expenditures on public services and capital investment by more than $5 million and still finish the year with a surplus of more than $200,000. Most of this increased service was made possible by a dramatic improvement in the local economy, which accounts for the $2.4 million increase in sales tax receipts, replacing the property tax as the city's major revenue source.
>
>   The General Fund summary shows that your city government is continuing the emphasis of the last two years on improving public safety. Support for the Police Department, which increased by $800,000 last year, is up by another $200,000-plus in the budget adopted by the City Council for this fiscal year. In the wake of a series of management changes in the past year, budget support for the Fire Department is also being increased significantly.

Your instructor will portray the city manager and hold a news conference to discuss the year-end financial statement. Prepare at least five written questions in advance. Then write the story.

17. Using the Internet, find the sales tax for Colorado and New York. How many percentage points difference is there? What percent difference is it?

18. CHALLENGE EXERCISE

As Springfield has become a more attractive place to live and as business has grown, people have watched their property values increase. The millage rate, 18.75, has remained the same since 1996.

a. Calculate how much property taxes went up for the median home in Springfield, which the property appraiser valued at $100,000 in 1996 and at $150,000 in 2012.

b. Adjust the tax and property value figures for inflation, and calculate how much property values and property taxes have increased in real dollars.

The Inverted Pyramid

1. The six questions that journalists traditionally ask themselves when categorizing information for leads are who, what, where, when, why, and how. For each of the following leads, identify the answers to these questions. Then indicate which two questions the writer believes to be the most important.

   A. NEW YORK—A scientist dismissed from an Environmental Protection Agency panel on secondhand cigarette smoke after vigorous lobbying by the tobacco industry says he will fight to be reinstated.
      a. Who?

      b. What?

      c. Where?

      d. When?

      e. Why?

      f. How?

      g. Which does the writer believe are the two most important questions in this lead?
         1.
         2.

   B. Springfield police arrested a local woman Thursday for allegedly filing a false police report of a rape last month.
      a. Who?

      b. What?

c. Where?

d. When?

e. Why?

f. How?

g. Which does the writer believe are the two most important questions in this lead?
1.
2.

C. The United Way Board of Directors will announce how it plans to allocate $425,000 when it meets at 2 p.m. tomorrow at the board's offices.
a. Who?

b. What?

c. Where?

d. When?

e. Why?

f. How?

g. Which does the writer believe are the two most important questions in this lead?
1.
2.

D. After 400 students protested a proposed tuition increase at Springfield University on Friday, university President Michael R. Quinn agreed to reconsider his recommendation.
a. Who?

b. What?

c. Where?

d. When?

e. Why?

f. How?

g. Which does the writer believe are the two most important questions in this lead?
   1.
   2.

2. Here are the leads for the same news as they appeared on three different websites.

A. FTC Press Release

The Federal Trade Commission announced that Skechers USA, Inc. has agreed to pay $40 million to settle charges that the company deceived consumers by making unfounded claims that Shape-ups would help people lose weight, and strengthen and tone their buttocks, legs and abdominal muscles.

Besides Shape-ups, Skechers also made deceptive claims about its Resistance Runner, Toners, and Tone-ups shoes, the FTC alleged. Consumers who bought these "toning" shoes will be eligible for refunds either directly from the FTC or through a court-approved class action lawsuit, and can submit a claim here. The settlement with the FTC is part of a broader agreement, also being announced today resolving a multi-state investigation, which was led by the Tennessee and Ohio Attorneys General Offices and included attorneys general from 42 other states and the District of Columbia.

B. Associated Press

WASHINGTON—The government wants you to know that simply sporting a pair of Skechers' fitness shoes is not going to get you Kim Kardashian's curves or Brooke Burke's toned tush.

Skechers USA Inc. will pay $40 million to settle charges by the Federal Trade Commission that the footwear company made unfounded claims that its Shape-ups shoes would help people lose weight and strengthen their butt, leg and stomach muscles. Kardashian, Burke and other celebrities endorsed the shoes in Skechers ads.

C. Usatoday.com

The Federal Trade Commission said Wednesday that Skechers agreed to pay $40 million to settle charges it misled consumers with claims that its toning sneakers would do everything from help them lose weight to make their "bottom half their better half" without ever going to a gym.

The settlement, which will be used to provide refunds to buyers of Shape-ups and other Skechers toning sneakers, is believed to be the FTC's largest ever involving consumer refunds, says David Vladeck, director of the FTC's Bureau of Consumer Protection.

a. Which of the three leads answers more of the six questions basic to all stories? Which questions does it answer?

b. What is the first question answered in each of the three leads?
   A.
   B.
   C.

c. Which is the best lead, and why?

3. Search the Internet for three stories on the same subject published on the same day. For each story, identify the answers to the seven basic questions (who, what, where, when, why, how, and so what). How many paragraphs do you have to read to find the answers? If the "so what" is missing, can you figure out what it should be?

4. Here are leads for the same story as they appeared in three newspapers:

A. WASHINGTON—The USA's 40 million Social Security recipients will get an unexpected benefit from inflation: fatter checks.

B. WASHINGTON—The nation's 40 million Social Security beneficiaries will receive a 5.4 percent cost-of-living increase in January, the biggest boost in more than eight years, the government announced Thursday.

C. WASHINGTON—The nation's 40 million Social Security recipients will receive their biggest increase in 8 1/2 years in January, a 5.4 percent increase that will average an extra $31 a month.

a. Which of the three leads answers more of the six questions basic to all stories? Which questions does it answer?

b. What is the first question answered in each of the three leads?
   A.
   B.
   C.

c. Which is the best lead, and why?

d. Write a "you" lead based on the information in the three leads.

5. Here are the facts: The Springfield University Faculty Council approved a plan Monday to convert to plus/minus grading from the standard A/B/C/D/F plan in existence. At other universities that have adopted the system, students' grade-point averages declined. The proposal will go to the university provost for final action.

Write a lead for your campus newspaper to emphasize this story's relevance to your readers.

6. Here are the facts: The university provost has announced that beginning next semester, students will be able to buy their books from the university bookstore online. Unless they are on probation, students will no longer have to obtain advisers' signatures.

Write a lead for your campus newspaper to emphasize the story's usefulness and relevance to your readers.

7. a. Write an immediate-identification lead of 35 words or fewer using the information given below.

b. Using the same information, write a delayed-identification lead of 35 words or fewer.

WHO: Duane La Chance, 55, Springfield, a pipe fitter employed by Gross Co. Engineers, a company based in Springfield

WHAT: Suffered third-degree burns and was listed in serious condition Tuesday night in the intensive-care unit at Springfield Hospital

WHERE: Springfield Municipal Power Plant, 222 Power Drive

WHEN: 3 p.m. Tuesday

HOW: La Chance was installing new pipes on the roof of the power plant when he accidentally touched a power line carrying 15,000 volts with a piece of angle iron.

SOURCE: Henry Rosen, project manager for Gross Co. Engineers

8. Using the following information, write the lead for a news story.

WHO: About 1,000 high school students

WHAT: Protest that turned into a rock- and bottle-throwing melee. Ten people were arrested, and nearly 30 were injured.

WHERE: Outside Montwood High School in your community

WHEN: Thursday

WHY: Students were protesting changes in class schedules, the student body president said.

HOW: Students walked out of class in protest and then began attacking security personnel with rocks and glass bottles.

9. a. Using the information provided below, write an immediate-identification lead of fewer than 35 words.

b. Using the same information, write a delayed-identification lead of fewer than 35 words.

WHO: James W. Cunning, 20, 505 W. Stewart Road, and Wayne Clay, 19, Route 1, Springfield

WHERE: On U.S. 63, one-tenth of a mile north of Blue Ridge Road

WHEN: 11:45 p.m. Saturday

WHAT AND HOW: Cunning was driving south on U.S. 63 in a 1994 Chevrolet; Clay was driving north in a 1992 Ford. Clay apparently crossed the center line and struck Cunning's vehicle, according to an officer in the Lincoln County Sheriff's Department. Cunning is in satisfactory condition at Springfield Hospital.

10. Using the following information, write an immediate-identification lead of fewer than 35 words.

WHO: Spc. Leslie H. Sabo Jr.

WHAT: Posthumously awarded a Medal of Honor by President Barack Obama

WHERE: At a White House ceremony

WHY: For heroism during combat in Cambodia. Though wounded, he charged an enemy bunker and destroyed it with a grenade. He died in the explosion.

WHEN: Yesterday

11. Assume that you are writing for your newspaper's website. Using the following information, write a lead for immediate publication.

WHO: Amtrak train called the Colonial

WHAT: Collided with three Conrail locomotives on a switch that merges four tracks into two

WHERE:	Near Chase, Md.
WHEN:	1:30 p.m. today
WHY:	Larry Case, Amtrak spokesman: The Conrail diesels, like the Amtrak, were northbound. The Conrail had apparently run a stop sign.
OTHER:	At least 15 dead, 175 injured. Worst accident in Amtrak's history.

12. An announcement came at the end of a news conference at Springfield City Hall yesterday. Mayor Juanita Williams was asked whether she had decided to run as a candidate for re-election. Williams said that she would not. She said she would support First Ward Council Member Hong Xiang.
   a. Write a tweet (140 characters or less) from the conference about the announcement.

   b. Write a lead for the website story.

   c. Now write a lead for the next morning's newspaper.

13. There are several topics on the agenda of the Springfield City Council tomorrow night. One is the proposed approval of an agreement negotiated with Local 45, which represents 90 percent of city workers. It provides for a 4 percent pay increase. Another is action on a proposed ordinance that would restrict commercial signs in the downtown district. Yet another is an ordinance regulating the amount of noise permitted. It was requested by residents who live near fraternity and sorority houses. As always, the council meets at 7 p.m. at City Hall.
   a. Write the advance for your city newspaper's website.

   b. Write a lead for tomorrow morning's campus paper.

14. The Springfield Board of Education met Monday night. Superintendent Max Schmidt reported that enrollment was 17 more than expected but that there were no other problems associated with last week's school opening. Schmidt said he would be negotiating with the Maintenance Workers Union next week. He said they have already agreed on binding

arbitration if necessary. He then presented the board with a revision to the school manual. This is the first time the manual has been revised in 20 years, he said. "It's overdue. There have been several changes in the law and the mores that we must recognize."

Board member Janet Biss said she opposed several of the changes. She particularly did not like giving students permission to wear shorts, to drive their cars to school and to carry cellphones. "These rules were good enough for my generation; they're good enough for the students now." Other changes were that teachers could not use their private email to communicate with students, teachers must report all violations of school policy to the building principal, students convicted of using any kind of drug will be suspended for no more than 20 days, and all students found with drugs in the school will be turned over to juvenile authorities.

The board voted 5-2 to approve the new manual. Student Body President Ryan Rodriguez said he welcomed the school board to the 21st century. The board then accepted a low bid from Farmer's Dairy to provide milk at 10 cents a pint.

a. Write a summary lead for the high school newspaper using the preceding information.

b. Write a summary lead for the daily newspaper's website using the preceding information.

c. Write a multiple-element lead for the school newspaper using the same information.

d. Write a multiple-element lead for the daily's website using the same information.

e. Write a "you" lead for the daily's website.

15. The two candidates for mayor debated last night at the high school. The debate was sponsored by the League of Women Voters. About 245 people attended. More than 300 were expected. Republican candidate Jesse Abraham said he would try to accomplish three things if elected: (1) He would widen and improve Main Street; (2) he would buy land to build a city park on the south side; and (3) he would streamline council meetings.

Democratic candidate Juanita Williams, the incumbent, accused Abraham of logrolling. She said he was trying to give something to everyone. "The city tax base can't support the kinds of programs he is proposing," she said. She also revealed that she has learned that Abraham's largest contributors are merchants who own land along Main Street. "They're the only ones who would benefit from widening the street," she charged. Abraham said he had not received a single donation from the merchants. Questioned from the audience, he said he would not make public the names of campaign donors until after the election on Nov. 3.

League President Sally Harm thanked the candidates for a good debate and said she thought the evening was a success.

a. Write a tweet (140 characters or less) from the debate based on the preceding information.

b. Write a summary lead using the preceding information.

c. Write a multiple-element lead using the same information.

16. Using the following information, write a lead with a twist.

> Gary Roets, 49, 6204 Ridge Road, and Duane Craig, 51, 6206 Ridge Road, collided when they backed out of their driveways Tuesday morning. Both were on their way to work. Damage to the Roets vehicle was estimated at $250; to the Craig vehicle, about $400. Information is from the Springfield police.

17. Identify the "so what" information in the following excerpt. Is it sufficient? Explain.

> Terry Woolworth lost her health and her car after a drunken driver smashed into her last December. Unable to work, she then lost her business and her house.
>
> Now she has lost confidence in the legal system.
>
> The 35-year-old Detroit woman learned recently that the drunken driver who hit her—and who now has at least five alcohol-related convictions—had his six-month jail sentence in her case overturned and never served a day behind bars.
>
> "This has destroyed my life, and the justice system has treated it like a joke," Woolworth said. "My God, look at his record, and he's still out on the streets."
>
> Woolworth is one of many who regularly lose in a drunken-driving numbers game that is stacked against public safety, some judges say.
>
> Woolworth's case lends weight to the debate about how Detroit's chronic drunken drivers should be handled when they enter the justice system.

18. Use the Internet to find three news stories on the same subject from different sources, such as a staff version, an Associated Press version, a *New York Times* version, a CNN version, and so on. Count the number of words

in each of the first three paragraphs. Which version is easiest to understand? Which answers the seven questions? What are the differences in news judgment among them?

19. Using your *Associated Press Stylebook* or the abbreviated version of it found in Appendix 2 of your textbook, correct the following for style errors.

Springfield University President Michael Quinn said today that he will recommend to the Board of Curators that tuition be increased by 6% each of the next two years.

The Curators meet at 10 a.m. Friday morning in room 249 Student Union, 322 University Avenue.

Springfield Student Association President Milo Nishada said he would oppose the recommendation. "The University is trying to balance the budget on the backs of students, and it's not fair," he said.

20. Read the following information, and do the exercises that follow.

Springfield police were called to the corner of Ninth and Elm streets at 4:30 p.m. Monday to investigate a two-car accident. After arriving, they called for an ambulance because two people had been injured. Two people were believed dead. Witnesses told police that the car in which the injured persons were riding was heading south on Ninth Street and went through a red light. It hit the other car broadside. The other car rolled over three times and came to rest against a light pole.

At the hospital, the victims were identified as James and Martha Westhaver. James was 55. His wife was 60. James Westhaver was president of the Merchants National Bank, the largest bank in Springfield. Injured were James West, 43, and Samuel Blackwater, 32, both city employees in the Parks and Recreation Department. West suffered a broken leg and possible concussion; Blackwater had two broken arms and a broken nose.

Police ticketed West for careless and imprudent driving. But Prosecuting Attorney James Taylor said he would investigate before determining whether involuntary manslaughter charges should be lodged against West. A bank official said Westhaver had been employed there for 33 years. He was also chairman of the United Way this year and treasurer of the Chamber of Commerce. His wife hosted a talk show on KTGG, a local television station. Funeral arrangements are incomplete.

a. Write a news story using the inverted-pyramid style. Use the type of lead you think is appropriate.

b. Write a short, quick version to post immediately on your newspaper's website.

21. Monica Drummond, 26, of 4527 W. Fourth St., and Jim Poplar, 28, of 5642 N. 11th St., were arrested on burglary charges. Police said the two broke into 14 houses in three neighborhoods over a 23-day period and made off with 200 items valued at $43,000.
   a. Identify which numbers you would use later in the story and which you would eliminate completely.

   b. Write a lead focusing on the most important elements.

22. Using the following information, complete the exercises that follow.

   Four o'clock this morning, one day before the opening of the racing season. Lincoln Downs Race Track, Springfield. A fire in a barn where 25 horses were stabled. Dead are 15 horses: 13 thoroughbred and two saddle horses. Ten escaped, including two that stampeded through the barnyard with their backs on fire. Arson is suspected as the cause. The barn had been a one-story wooden structure. Only several rows of charred wooden supports remain after the fire. An arson squad has been called to the scene. The fire smoldered until noon. A jockey, Albert Ramos, of Miami, Fla., watched workers as they cleaned up the area. "Those are my best friends," he said, pointing to the surviving horses. "I love horses more than I do people. I feel like I want to cry."

   Statements from officials: Dan Bucci, assistant general manager of the track: "It could have been of an incendiary nature because it started in the middle of the barn, not at the end. The only heaters and electrical outlets were in the tack rooms at the ends of the barn."

   Bernard Perry, fire chief: "The fire exploded near the center of the barn. Flames were shooting out of the building when we got here. The fire is definitely suspicious."

   a. Write a news story using the inverted-pyramid style.
   b. Suggest possible links and sidebars for the online story.

23. **CHALLENGE EXERCISE**
   Read the following information. Then do the exercises that follow.

   Randy Cohen, Christy Wapniarski, Daniel Perrin, Tammy Ennis—all students at Springfield University—went sailing near Daytona Beach, Fla., yesterday in a 16-foot catamaran. About 5 p.m. the boat sprang a leak and capsized. The four hung on to one of the catamaran's pontoons through the night. They were wearing no life jackets, and the Atlantic Ocean's current was strong.

   At dawn they decided to swim to shore at Ormond Beach 4 miles away. Randy Cohen, 19, was about 20 feet in front of Christy Wapniarski, 19, when he heard her call for help. She said a shark had attacked her. Cohen called to Ennis, who was 10 feet ahead of him, to help, but she yelled, "Randy, don't go back there; you'll get eaten too."

By the time Cohen had swum back to Wapniarski, she was unconscious, and he could see no sign of a shark. He put his arms around her shoulders and began swimming for shore. Perrin, 20, had been swimming behind the other three. He swam to the aid of Cohen and Wapniarski and checked her pulse. He told Cohen that Wapniarski was dead, but Cohen refused to let go. He swam with her another 15 or 20 minutes until he was exhausted; then he let her go.

It took the three students six more hours to reach shore. Cohen was stung by dozens of Portuguese man-of-wars. He is in Halifax Hospital, Daytona Beach. The others were examined at the hospital and released. You, as the reporter, talked to Cohen by phone in his hospital room.

a. Write a quick, one-paragraph account for your newspaper's website.
b. With the same information, write a news story using the inverted-pyramid style.
c. Suggest ideas for links, sidebars and visuals for the online version of the story.

Beyond the Inverted Pyramid

7

1. Reporters need to use all of their senses to report. Examine stories in newspapers, in magazines or on the Web, and find at least one example of reporting with each of the senses. Evaluate what the reporting added to the story.

2. Write five sentences, each demonstrating facts gathered with one of the five senses.

3. The following story is written in the news narrative structure. Identify the numbered parts of the structure by function.

By John Tully
Columbia Missourian

(1) About five months ago, Cara Walker, 17, was lying in a hospital recovering from the spinal injury she received when she lost control of her car, rolled the vehicle and was thrown halfway through the side window.

Doctors weren't sure she would ever ride again. **(2)** On Sunday, in a remarkable turnaround, Walker competed in the Midway Fall Classic Quarter Horse Show at the Midway Expo Center. **(3)** The results were surprising.

(4) Last July, Walker, a junior at Rock Bridge High School, was taking a lunch break from riding in preparation for the Fort Worth Invitational, where she qualified in five events. Driving with three passengers on a back road near Moberly, she rolled her car at 50 mph where the paved road turned to gravel without warning. Walker was the only one not wearing a seat belt. Her head and upper body smashed through the side window.

Fortunately, she was still in her riding boots. Her spurs got caught on the bar under the seat, which Walker says may have saved her life.

At the time of the accident, Walker was nationally ranked in the trail-riding event.

Doctors fused her neck in surgery. During the next couple of weeks, she was able to shed her full upper-body cast. Walker returned home to her parents and twin sisters two days after surgery, but her mother, Jane Walker, said doctors told her to stay away from her sport for a few months until she healed.

For Walker, the top all-around youth rider in Missouri and the president of the American Quarter Horse Youth Association, the four months following the accident was her first time away from riding.

After returning home she worked to regain strength and mobility from the accident that initially left her right side paralyzed. She walked short distances. Going to the mailbox at the end of the driveway wore her out, her mother recalls.

Walker had to work almost every muscle in her body back into shape. After the accident, the family brought her 10-year-old quarter horse to their barn in Columbia. That motivated Walker to at first walk to the barn and then to start caring for the horse and eventually ride again.

(5) Sunday, the rehabilitation was complete. With ramrod posture and strict horse control, she won first place in the horsemanship class.

4. In each of the following focus structure examples, identify whether the writer is using an anecdotal lead, a scene re-creation or another kind of lead by circling the appropriate phrase and noting the type of lead in the margin. Then mark the transition and theme paragraphs in the story.

A. After 10 years at System Planning Corp. in Arlington, Sandra Wong had risen to the rank of administrative assistant, was earning a $40,000 salary and had just agreed to buy a townhouse. She was a seasoned professional.

So when her boss told her in August that she had been "surplused," she first thought she was being promoted.

Hardly. She was being laid off.

Unemployed, Wong could not go through with the townhouse purchase. Because she had already sold her condominium, she had to move into a rented apartment. Now, she must start job hunting.

Wong and thousands of professionals like her give a distinctive, white-collar shading to the ranks of Washington's unemployed.

As defense, real estate, retail and financial companies have laid off workers and otherwise shrunk their staffs, a growing class of unemployed managers, consultants, engineers, architects and real estate agents has emerged.

B. Fire in the Hole

Raging in mines from Pennsylvania to China, coal fires threaten towns, poison air and water, and add to global warming.

By Kevin Krajick
Smithsonian

From the back kitchen window of his little house on a ridge in east-central Pennsylvania, John Lokitis looks out on a most unusual prospect. Just uphill, at the edge of St. Ignatius Cemetery, the earth is ablaze. Vegetation has been obliterated along a quarter-mile strip; sulfurous steam billows out of hundreds of fissures and holes in the mud. There are pits extending perhaps 20 feet down: in their depths, discarded plastic bottles and tires have melted. Dead trees, their trunks bleached white, lie in tangled heaps, stumps venting smoke through hollow centers. Sometimes fumes seep across the cemetery fence to the grave of Lokitis' grandfather, George Lokitis.

This hellish landscape constitutes about all that remains of the once-thriving town of Centralia, Pennsylvania. Forty-three years ago, a vast honeycomb of coal mines at the edge of the town caught fire. An underground inferno has been spreading ever since, burning at depths of up to 300 feet, baking surface layers, venting poisonous gases and opening holes large enough to swallow people or cars. The conflagration may burn for another 250 years, along an eight-mile stretch encompassing 3,700 acres, before it runs out of the coal that fuels it.

C. NEW YORK—By all accounts, it was the happiest day in the largely unhappy life of Joanne Bashold; not in all her 24 years had her family ever heard her so exuberant.

"I had a baby girl yesterday," Joanne announced on Sept. 2 from a pay telephone somewhere in New York's Bellevue Hospital. Her younger sister Barbara, receiving the call at the Bashold residence in Kirtland, Ohio, was astonished. The family hadn't known Joanne was pregnant and wasn't even sure where she was.

"How are you?" Barbara asked. But Joanne wanted only to talk about her baby girl, Cara. "She has tons of black hair. She's so little and so cute."

Four days after that conversation took place, the baby was dead. It was devoured and killed by a starving German shepherd, Joanne's own pet and sole companion in the East Harlem slum she called home.

As a result, Joanne was charged with criminally negligent homicide. But last Thursday, the charge was dropped at the request of the District Attorney's office. "We concluded there was no purpose to be served by prosecuting her," District Attorney Robert M. Morgenthau said.

Her story is the story of how a young woman—like so many thousands of other young women in this country—came to New York to find herself but was overwhelmed by a city where anonymity is worn like a badge.

It is a story of a woman from a small town with gentle, undulating hills where neighbors help each other—a woman who fell through the cracks of a complicated bureaucratic system that is supposed to aid people like her.

5. Find a story organized in a manner other than the inverted pyramid. Indicate the type of opening, and identify the transition and theme paragraphs.

6. Is the opening of the following story exposition or narration? How do you know? Also identify the nut paragraph and the foreshadowing.

During his years as America's noisiest preacher, Billy James Hargis likened himself to the Old Testament prophet Ezekiel—a "watchman on the wall" ordered to "blow the trumpet" of warning against sin and evil.

And could he ever wail on that horn. In the fifties, the Tulsa evangelist launched a "Christian Crusade" against communism. His crusading culture warriors, including Youth Director David A. Noebel, climbed to the ramparts to sound one continuous air-raid siren against the barbarians at the gate.

In the process, Hargis, an imposing man with the physique of Oliver Hardy and the lung power of Ethel Merman, scared up enough money to travel the globe and amass fancy homes, summer retreats and expensive paintings.

No other preacher of his era possessed Hargis' combination of salesmanship, charm, fear-mongering and oratory, which decades ago earned him the label "doomsday merchant on the far right" and today a reputation as one of the century's most effective orators.

And no other preacher self-destructed so spectacularly.

7. Is the opening to the following story exposition or narration? How do you know?

Connie Pitts' voice quavers as she speaks into the emergency room radio. She has repeated the lines calmly many times before—but always to begin drills. "This is Deaconess Medical Center calling all Spokane area hospitals. This is your hospital control center. This is a disaster call."

Playing in Pitts' mind is the horrific warning just relayed to the hospital from a lieutenant at Fairchild Air Force Base: "We've got five . . . 12 . . . 17 wounded and two dead. They're all gunshot wounds."

Five nurses and Greg Jones, the only doctor in the emergency room, look at each other in disbelief.

8. The following story contains dialogue.

> The entry wound is deceiving, as if a pencil punctured the skin. The exit wound is jagged and deep. Bambino has seen nothing this gory—not even the patient with a hatchet buried in his back.
>
> "I'll bet it was an AK-47," says Russell Oakley, an orthopedic surgeon.
>
> Sam's voice surprises the doctors: "I thought it was an M-16."
>
> The boy is talking, but Bambino sees terror in his eyes. "I'm scared," he says. "Am I going to die?"
>
> Bambino, thrilled that Sam can wiggle his toes, tells him he will live. "Just squeeze my hand when it hurts, and hold still."

a. What does the writer do to re-create the dialogue? How does the dialogue change the scene for the reader?

b. Rewrite this example, using traditional journalistic quotations. Which is better, dialogue or quotations, and why?

9. In the following excerpt, circle the concrete details the writer uses to re-create the scene she saw.

> Billy Ross Sims is handcuffed and sweating. Not an easy combination.
>
> As perspiration beads up on his forehead, then drips into his eyebrows, Sims—afraid of losing his train of thought, his rant—dips his head down to clear away the sweat by dragging his face across the lap of his white prison overalls.
>
> His head darts back up, and it's as though he never stopped talking. Talking and grimacing, talking and sweating—working himself up into an anguished frenzy, determined to recall and relay every detail of the interminably long story of his wrongful imprisonment.

Can you see Sims? Is it as if you were watching a video? Take out the concrete details. How much information is left?

10. A college student wrote this opening to a story about victims of a California earthquake. What does the foreshadowing promise? Does it make you want to read more of the story?

> The October afternoon was warm and muggy, and although no such thing exists, people called it perfect earthquake weather. Ruth Rabinowitz was anticipating a night out with her lover, Robin Ortiz, when they met at 4 p.m. at the Santa Cruz Coffee Roasting Company. "We had a date that night for dinner and a show," says Rabinowitz.
>
> Rabinowitz, a production manager at the company, had to work an extra hour that Tuesday evening preparing orders for the next day. Before leaving, she gave Ortiz a hug. It was the last time she would see her alive.

11. Find an example of foreshadowing, and evaluate its effectiveness.

12. Circle the "so what" in the following story opening.

Whites Account for Under Half of Births in U.S.
By Sabrina Tavernise
The New York Times

WASHINGTON—After years of speculation, estimates and projections, the Census Bureau has made it official: White births are no longer a majority in the United States.

Non-Hispanic whites accounted for 49.6 percent of all births in the 12-month period that ended last July, according to Census Bureau data made public on Thursday, while minorities—including Hispanics, blacks, Asians and those of mixed race—reached 50.4 percent, representing a majority for the first time in the country's history.

Such a turn has been long expected, but no one was certain when the moment would arrive—signaling a milestone for a nation whose government was founded by white Europeans and has wrestled mightily with issues of race, from the days of slavery, through a civil war, bitter civil rights battles and, most recently, highly charged debates over efforts to restrict immigration.

While overall, whites will remain a majority for some time, the fact that a younger generation is being born in which minorities are the majority has broad implications for the country's economy, its political life and its identity. "This is an important tipping point," said William H. Frey, the senior demographer at the Brookings Institution, describing the shift as a "transformation from a mostly white baby boomer culture to the more globalized multiethnic country that we are becoming."

Signs that the country is evolving this way start with the Oval Office, and have swept hundreds of counties in recent years, with 348 in which whites are no longer in the majority. That number doubles when it comes to the toddler population, Mr. Frey said. Whites are no longer the majority in four states and the District of Columbia, and have slipped below half in many major metro areas, including New York, Las Vegas and Memphis.

13. Using your campus newspaper website or any other news source, find two examples of "so what" paragraphs and one story in memo format. Post the items on your journalism blog, evaluating the effectiveness of each.

14. Using the focus structure, write about three paragraphs on the following information:

    There are 20,000 injuries in high school football each year—12 percent of them permanently disabling the victims. Thirteen youths died last year. Thirty-five percent of the injuries are to the neck or head. Most critics blame the helmet. Pete Stenhoff, 16, a junior at Chula Vista High School in Redmond, Calif., was hurt in a game during his junior year. He rammed his head into the ball carrier's chest. Stenhoff cracked vertebrae in his spine and now is confined to a wheelchair for life. At the time of the accident he weighed 210 pounds; now he weighs 172 pounds. He didn't graduate with his class and is trying to get his diploma by taking correspondence courses. He is not bitter. "I knew the risks involved when I decided to play football," he says, and adds, "but I wish I would have known just how bad it could be."

15. Using the focus structure, write about three paragraphs on the following information:

    Thirty years ago, Rosemary Morris and her sister, Emma, went to a cattle show in Ohio to look at some Dexters. Dexters are an Irish breed now on the endangered list of the American Livestock Breed Conservancy. The sisters were interested in expanding their small herd. Rosemary met another Dexter herd owner, Dean Fleharty, then living in Iowa. They found not only more Dexters but also love. They married and settled on a small farm in Missouri.

    Dexters live long, grow slowly and are great milk producers. In this day when the emphasis is on beef, most breeders prefer other breeds. It takes more than two years for a Dexter to reach market weight; it takes six months of corn and grain byproducts to bring the more popular breeds to market. That's why Dexters are unpopular. Breeders make more money raising other breeds that grow faster and are more uniform. The Dexter breed is not for mass production. Just three breeds—Angus, Hereford and Simmentals—now dominate 60 percent of American beef cattle. Dexter numbers have improved enough to be moved to the ALBC's recovering species list.

16. A soft lead uses an anecdote, a quotation or another literary device to draw in the reader. Write a soft opening of two or three paragraphs based on the following information.

    There are 55 million women in the country who work. Lillian Garland worked at California Federal Savings & Loan. She was granted a pregnancy leave. When she wanted to return, she was not given her job back. She sued under a California law requiring employers to grant up to four months' unpaid disability leave to pregnant workers and to guarantee a job for them when they return. The U.S. Supreme Court voted 6 to 2 Tuesday to uphold the state law. The ruling came five years after Garland had her baby.

17. Write about a memorable moment in your life as an anecdotal introduction to a story about how you came to be the person you are today. Continue through the transitional paragraph.

18. Find and evaluate two anecdotes from a newspaper or magazine—print or digital version. How effective are the anecdotes in engaging and holding your interest?

19. What are the service journalism aspects of a story about an upcoming City Council meeting? How would you make the story useful to readers?

20. Assume that you are devoting a couple of pages in your campus newspaper to information freshmen need to know when they arrive on your campus.

    a. Using a service journalism emphasis, create a story list and description. Then identify the parts of the information that would be presented in text, in lists and in other formats. Identify those formats.

    b. Now think about putting that and additional information on your campus website. What can you do on the Web that you cannot do in print?

21. CHALLENGE EXERCISE

In the excerpt that follows, the writer, a college student, has re-created an event he attended. In a one-page response, identify and analyze the writing techniques he used to take readers to the scene.

> While roosters face off in the "pit," opponents and supporters of cockfighting throughout the state clash in their views about whether the legal sport is a rural tradition or simply a game of cruelty.
>
> On a warm and sunny Saturday afternoon in April, the massive red barn outside Middletown begins to stir with activity. Pickup trucks turn slowly onto the gravel driveway. The entrance to the barn is prominently marked with two posts displaying statues of roosters. A sign on the barn reads "H & H Poultry."
>
> It's been two weeks since the last cockfight. Twice a month, cockers and fans gather to witness this long-standing tradition. Supporters of cockfighting see this ritual as a cultural event involving fighting roosters, while opponents view it as a cruel massacre and blood sport between animals forced to fight to the death.
>
> Inside the barn, the smell of country cooking permeates the air. A restaurant featuring homemade corn dogs and apple pies does a brisk business. Families sit at tables drinking soda and bantering.
>
> The barn is immaculate. At least 200 seats rise above the pit, the 20-square-foot area made of wood and surrounded on each side by wire. This is the ring in which the feathered combatants will face one another. The pit is covered in a mixture of dirt, peat moss and cottonseed hulls. It has been raked to perfection like the infield of a baseball diamond.
>
> An announcer's box sits high above the pit on the far end of the arena. Each side of the barn displays large red letters stating "Absolutely No Gambling." Each row in the arena has several empty canisters for patrons to discard their cigarette ashes and chewing tobacco. Behind the stands, several rooms house the fighting cocks, which alert everyone to their presence by continually crowing.
>
> It's 4 p.m., time for weigh-in.
>
> The roosters, Red Hatch and Calcutta Gray Battle Cross breeds, are placed on the scales. Once the weights are ascertained, they are entered into a computer that matches opponents down to the ounce. This ensures that weight will not give any rooster an unfair advantage over an opponent.
>
> Cockers—the men who own, raise and sometimes handle the birds during fights—have come from all over this Saturday night for the Missouri

State Championship. The defending champion, Ron Griffin of Hannibal, has brought his prize roosters.

As 6 p.m. approaches, excitement mounts among the cockers and the crowd. The seats alongside the pit fill up rapidly. Across the pit, several high school students, sporting their letter jackets, occupy the front row, laughing and joking. Three young children chase each other up and down the aisles, firing spitballs through their soda straws.

A man at the north end of the arena writes down the names of the fighting cocks on a large board. Each cock will fight once.

The hour has arrived. Two handlers emerge from under a tunnel, each holding a bird. Immediately, the people in the crowd begin making wagers with one another. "Five dollars on the white shirt," yells one man, referring to the white shirt of one of the handlers. "Ten on the red hat," yells another spectator, deciding to back the other handler, who dons a red ball cap.

As the handlers enter the pit, a referee draws chalk lines about eight feet apart in the middle of the ring. The handlers proceed toward the center. The majestic birds are Red Hatch Battle Crosses, possessing deep auburn plumage with streaks of blond, hairlike hackle feathers surrounding their necks. The roosters' amber spurs have been cut to a stump and replaced with 2 1/4-inch metal "gaffs," which are needlelike and curved at the ends.

Standing about two feet apart, the handlers hold the cocks within pecking distance of one another to stimulate their fighting instincts. Immediately, the birds begin pecking each other with voracious ire. The handlers separate, pulling one of the cocks' beaks from the other's head. The birds are now ready for the main bout.

Each handler steps behind one of the chalk lines in the center of the pit while maintaining a hold on his bird. The crowd cheers as the feathered gladiators prepare to do battle. The referee yells, "Pit!"

With hackle feathers swollen like umbrellas around their necks, the roosters dash toward each other with the ferocity of football linebackers. The birds clash in midair, wings flapping furiously. Feathers scatter in every direction. The battle rages on, until both become hung on the metal gaffs, prompting the referee to yell, "Handle that bird!"

The handlers pick up their birds, gently massaging their legs and blowing on their heads. Round two is about to begin. Once again, the birds charge one another, producing clicking noises as the razor-sharp gaffs penetrate their feathered bodies. This continues for five more rounds. Finally, one of the roosters begins to stagger, a victim of the sustained gaff punctures he has received during the fight.

The referee signals for the cockers to handle their birds, and the handler of the badly wounded rooster tries to "warm" the bird's head and body by blowing gently (a process cockers say helps increase circulation). In the next round, the wounded rooster refuses to stand up, resting squarely on his belly, apparently conceding defeat. The cockers, however, are not ready to end this clash.

The winning rooster continues to attack his ailing opponent, who miraculously rebounds to try and defend himself. By this time, the injured bird has lost all offensive capacity and rests on his side as blood drips from his beak. The referee begins a 10-count. By the time the referee reaches 10, the fatally wounded rooster falls lifelessly onto his side.

After 12 minutes of courageous fighting, it is over.

The handlers pick up their roosters and shake hands. For the winning bird, it's back to the cages behind the stands, where the cockers will scrutinize its body for injuries. For the loser, it's off to the incinerator in the back of the arena.

8 Writing News for Digital Media

1. Go to a newspaper or television station website. Study the site carefully, and critique it. Give specific examples of how the writing measures up to the following criteria for writing online.
   a. Do the news items reflect immediacy?

   b. Does the site attempt to save readers time?

   c. Does it provide information that's quick and easy to get?

   d. Does it provide information both visually and verbally?

e. Are the stories too long? Are they cut sufficiently?

f. Does the writing contain lists and bullets?

g. Are the stories broken into chunks?

h. Do the stories provide sufficient hyperlinks, both internal and external?

i. Is there ample opportunity for readers to respond?

j. Do the stories reflect "the human touch"—stressing what's important to readers?

2. Explain why online writers should present information in layers. Critique the performance of a website in that regard. Does it layer information, or does it present the information much as a newspaper would? Explain.

3. Why is it important to remember that "readers rule" online?

4. A teacher in a local elementary school has found a gun in a student's backpack. List at least six related stories you could write to accompany the primary story.

5. Rewrite the following stories for a newspaper website.
   a. After a long day, you get home from work and finally put dinner on the table. You're about to sit down and enjoy your pork chops and mashed potatoes when . . .

   Brring. Brring.

   "Hello, I am so and so from such and such. Would you like to buy . . . ?"

   That scene no longer must be part of the nightly ritual under a Senate bill the House passed Wednesday creating a state no-call list for telemarketers.

   The proposal, which must still acquire final approval of the Senate before being sent to the governor, allows up to a $5,000 civil penalty for any telemarketer who knowingly calls anyone on the no-call list. Anyone who receives more than one call from the same firm after being placed on the list can seek up to $5,000 for each violating call.

   The bill was passed unanimously, 118–0. The only critics were concerned that the bill would rob small businesses of important ways to make sales. But the bill's sponsor rejected that claim.

   "The question is, when does my telephone become an extension of your business?" said Rep. Don Wells, D-Springfield.

   Nonetheless, the critics succeeded in adding language exempting from the penalties businesses that make fewer than 100 such calls per week.

The measure, if passed in its current form, would not take effect until July. By January, the attorney general must have established a no-cost method for citizens to join the list.

Currently, citizens can avoid getting the calls by telling each telemarketer to place them on its no-call list. This bill seeks to fuse all the separate lists into one huge database.

The proposal also bans telemarketers from using technology that blocks Caller ID components on phones. It also requires any emailed marketing messages to include either a return email address or a toll-free 800 number citizens can use to tell the company to stop sending the messages.

In an unrelated development with even greater public policy ramifications, the Senate tabled a proposal that would place a tobacco money spending plan before the voters after anti-abortion language was added to the measure.

The language, part of the ongoing fight to ensure that no state money goes to abortions, brought a compromise attempt from the governor. He offered to sign an accompanying bill with softer anti-abortion language.

The conflict threatens to derail any decision on what to do with the pending tobacco money before the next crucial elections. At the beginning of the session, Governor Ramirez, who is running for the U.S. Senate, made spending the money on health projects one of his major priorities. If the plan is derailed, he will be deprived of an issue to trumpet in the campaign.

In an afternoon news conference, Ramirez was visibly agitated over the development.

"If we want to be a state that continuously litigates over abortions, let's get with it, but if we want good policy, let's do that," he said.

He was referring to the ongoing court battle between anti-abortion lawmakers and Planned Parenthood over whether state funds given to that group indirectly pay for abortions.

b. School board candidates are still on the campaign trail. Tuesday night they met at the Lenoir Retirement Community Center to address the concerns of senior citizens.

Unlike previous debates, where much of the discussion focused on the $35 million bond issue appearing on the April ballot, the bond was barely mentioned at all.

Instead, the senior citizens wanted to know about year-round schooling, what changes the candidates would enact and teacher unionization.

School board candidate Henry Lane said he believes there is "a changing tide" when it comes to using trailers as classrooms.

However, if year-round schooling were implemented, it would decrease the need for trailers, he said. Lane said a multitracking schedule would help overcrowding by reducing the number of students in daily attendance at the school by 25 percent.

Board President Elton Fay, also in the running, said year-round schooling isn't a practical idea.

"What Mr. Lane fails to tell you is that if we are to avoid erecting additional buildings, to save on construction costs, the cost of educating our children would go up substantially," Fay said.

Fay added that year-round schooling would mean different schedules for students of different ages.

"This community does not want schools on totally different schedules," he said.

Candidate Larry Dorman said that as a board member, he would focus on eliminating overcrowding in the schools and increasing teacher pay.

"If money weren't an issue, I'd build all the schools necessary," Dorman said.

Incumbent Kerry Corino said the increasing population makes it difficult to counteract large class sizes.

She said it is unfair to make comparisons between public and private schools because public schools cannot turn away students.

"Private schools can pick who they want; public schools cannot pick who they want," Corino said.

One senior citizen inquired as to whether teachers in the district can unionize.

Fay said teachers in this state cannot, by law, bargain collectively. He also said he doesn't support collective bargaining for teachers.

"The teachers are anti-union," Corino said. "That tells you a lot of things about how this city operates."

6. Online reporting can include sound, video and animation. Study a newspaper online, and identify several stories that might have been improved with sound, video or animation. Explain what the treatment would have added to the story. Also, find a site that does a good job of incorporating sound, video and animation, and explain why you think it succeeds.

7. Online writing expert Jakob Nielsen stresses the importance of credibility in online writing. He says it is often unclear where information comes from and whether it can be trusted. He notes, "Links to other sites show that the authors have done their homework and are not afraid to let readers visit other sites." Some online editors argue that you should not send readers away from the newspaper they are reading. Discuss both sides of this issue.

8. Choose a major breaking story in today's news. Visit five online news sites to compare the coverage. Choose the one you think provides the best coverage. Specifically, why did you choose the one you did?

9. Most newspapers, magazines and television stations now have blogs where reporters and editors can talk with readers, and readers can talk with one another. Find a blog on a local newspaper or television station website, and write a one- to two-page report analyzing it. What is the hottest topic on the blog?

10. Many series of lengthy newspaper articles are the result of an investigative reporting project, and those types of stories often are the ones that win Pulitzer Prizes. If you were the author of such a series, how would you suggest that the content be altered for the Web?

11. **CHALLENGE EXERCISE**
    Go to the website of the British Broadcasting Corp. (bbc.co.uk). Select a major story from that site, and make an inventory of how the BBC covered it. Look particularly for the number and types of stories written specifically to cover this event or issue, links to background material or external sources, audio, video and graphics. In a one- to two-page report, analyze what the BBC could have done better.

9 Writing News for Radio and Television

1. Watch a local evening newscast, and make a list of all the nonsports stories you see. Compare these stories with the ones on your local newspaper's website. Then answer the following questions:
   a. Which television stories do you think were selected primarily because of timeliness?
   b. Which television stories made you want to turn to the newspaper's website for more information?
   c. Which television stories do you think were chosen because of their visual impact? Do the Web versions have the same visual impact?

2. Following are three stories written for television and radio. Read them, and answer the following questions:
   a. Do the stories emphasize immediacy? If so, how?
   b. Are they written in a conversational style?
   c. Are they written tightly?
   d. Are they written clearly?

   A. FLAGSTAFF, Ariz. (AP)—A Flagstaff, Ariz., man who is suing the city is now its mayor.

   The Arizona Daily Sun reports (http://bit.ly/JrL3zQ) 63-year-old Jerry Nabours was elected mayor Tuesday night.

   The retired attorney beat City Councilman Al White by 320 votes in the vote-by-mail election.

   With more than 10,000 votes cast, turnout was about 39 percent.

   Nabours says his victory is a validation of his conservative fiscal vision for Flagstaff. He has criticized White's policies as a waste of taxpayer money as well as the city's public-private partnerships.

   Nabours is suing Flagstaff over an ordinance that requires property owners to pay for repairs of city-owned sidewalks. He initiated the suit in 2009 after receiving a $5,000 bill for a sidewalk in front of an apartment building he co-owns.

   The case is awaiting review in the Arizona Supreme Court.

   B. **Eight Dead, 61 Hurt as Explosions Rock New Delhi**
   NEW DELHI (AP)—At least eight people are dead and more than 60 injured after a series of explosions rocked New Delhi today.

   The mayor says as many as seven blasts went off, but authorities are still investigating.

   Police say the blasts appear to be coordinated. A Muslim militant group has claimed responsibility.

Two of the explosions occurred just 300 yards apart in the city's central business district. One went off by a metro station entrance on a major road. A police officer at the scene says a bomb appeared to have been left inside a trash can. The sidewalk was covered with scattered garbage, broken glass and a bright red pool of blood.

A store clerk, who was nearby when he heard an explosion, says people "heard the bomb and they just started running."

C. ICC Probing Deadly Darfur Camp Attack

THE HAGUE, Netherlands (AP)—The chief prosecutor of the International Criminal Court says he is investigating an attack by Sudanese troops on a refugee camp that left dozens of civilians dead last month.

Luis Moreno-Ocampo says he is considering adding the attack to a list of allegations against Sudanese President Omar al-Bashir.

The Aug. 25 attack at Kalma camp reportedly left 32 people dead including women and children.

In July, Moreno-Ocampo asked judges to issue an arrest warrant for al-Bashir on genocide charges for allegedly leading a five-year campaign of murder and rape against civilians in Darfur.

Moreno-Ocampo said Friday he is trying to find out if the Kalma camp attack was an isolated incident or part of a new government policy.

3. Rewrite the following newspaper wire stories for both radio and television. Assume that you are writing for a Springfield radio or television station. Include ideas for video for each story.

a. Obama Boulevard Is Proposed in St. Louis

ST. LOUIS (AP)—St. Louis alderwoman Kacie Starr Triplett has proposed that the city's Delmar Boulevard receive the honorary name of Barack Obama Boulevard.

The proposal is co-sponsored by four other city aldermen and was set to be introduced last night at a St. Louis Board of Aldermen meeting. Triplett said Thursday that Delmar "has served as an unofficial line of racial demarcation in St. Louis" between north and south sections of the city.

She said the street still would be known as Delmar, but six signs would be posted to honor the president-elect.

b. Deputy State Treasurer to Be Circuit Trial Judge

JEFFERSON CITY (AP)—The deputy state treasurer will become a trial judge in south-central Missouri.

Gov. Matt Blunt has appointed Doug Gaston as an associate circuit judge in the 25th Judicial Circuit. The circuit covers Maries, Pulaski, Phelps and Texas counties.

The appointment was announced yesterday.

Gaston, 41, also has been a Republican state House member from Houston, Mo., and the Texas County prosecutor.

He lives in Jefferson City and has a bachelor's degree from Southwest Baptist University and a law degree from the University of Arkansas.

c. Expo 2012 to Open in Yeosu, South Korea

YEOSU, South Korea (AP)—Expo 2012 has opened in South Korea's coastal city of Yeosu for a three-month run.

Organizers say the fair, which kicked off Saturday, has the largest number of robots in the history of expos. Attractions include a robot fish that explores underwater resources in an environment-friendly way.

Organizers say about 33,000 tickets were sold for the opening day. More than 100 countries are participating in the expo to display their technology, culture and products.

Yeosu is a port city 300 kilometers (185 miles) south of Seoul. It has built a gigantic structure in the water to display colorful hologram images and promote the expo.

d. Husband, Wife Arrested on Burglary Charges

TROY (AP)—A husband and wife are accused of breaking into about 60 homes around rural eastern Missouri, stealing guns, jewelry and other valuables and then selling them to a jewelry store owner who sold the stolen goods over the Internet, authorities said Thursday.

All three—Kibb Patrick Howard, 27, Carla Kay Howard, 26, and Michael Carl Sifrit, 42—face multiple state charges, and authorities are seeking federal indictments, Lincoln County Lt. Andy Binder said Thursday at a news conference. The three are jailed in Warren County, where the first charges were filed.

Police said they found about 100 stolen weapons and other stolen property at Sifrit's home in Fenton. Three guns and stolen jewelry allegedly were found at his S&S Jewelers in Warrenton, which police described as a front for the illegal sale of stolen guns and other stolen property.

Lincoln County detective Shannon Bowen said investigators were looking into reports that Sifrit sold some of the items on eBay.

4. Assume that the following four stories will follow one another in a news broadcast in Los Angeles. Rewrite the leads, lead-ins and wrap-ups for these news items.

a. Fire Doused, Search for Victims Continues

LOS ANGELES (AP)—Firefighters have put out a fire under part of a Los Angeles train wreck that killed at least 10 people.

A commuter train carrying 222 people collided head-on with a freight train during the Friday afternoon rush. More than 100 people have been injured and an unknown number of others have been trapped in a passenger car crushed by its own engine.

Fire Chief Dennis Barry says firefighters are still in the "rescue and extrication phase," hours after the collision. He says heavy equipment is coming in to wrench the trains apart.

Assistant Police Chief James McDonnell says one of the dead is a Los Angeles police officer.

The cause of the collision is under investigation. It isn't clear how the two trains ended up heading toward each other on the same track.

There is a siding nearby where one train can wait for another to pass. An engineering expert says the stretch of track has had a reputation for trouble.

Mayor Antonio Villaraigosa (vee-yah-ry-GOH'-sah) says it's the worst accident he's ever seen.

b. Skinhead Slayings

MIDLAND, Mich. (AP)—Two teenage skinhead brothers have waived extradition from Michigan to Pennsylvania.

They'll face charges they murdered their parents and younger brother.

Seventeen-year-old Bryan Freeman and 16-year-old David Freeman appeared briefly today in a court in Midland, Mich. They gave subdued answers of "yes" and "no" to a judge's questions.

The brothers were arrested in Michigan two days after their family's bodies were found in their home near Allentown, Pa.

Their court-appointed lawyers say the teens are sorry about the deaths.

But the lawyers won't say if the boys confessed.

c. **Armored Cars**

LOS ANGELES (AP)—Some abortion clinic doctors want more than handguns for protection; they're buying armored cars.

A company that adds armored plating to cars says physicians throughout California and the country are buying bullet-proof vehicles.

Five people have been killed in abortion clinic shootings since 1993.

A spokesman for the O'Gara-Hess and Eisenhardt Armoring Company says after the Massachusetts abortion clinics shootings in December, they received 39 phone calls that produced three sales.

The cost of converting a conventional car to an armored one can run from a few thousand dollars to $150,000.

That top-end price turns a Cadillac Eldorado into a vehicle guaranteed to repel armor-piercing shells. Options include pistol ports, thick glass and tear gas jets in wheel wells.

d. **L.A. Serial Killer Could Be Connected to Other Cases**

LOS ANGELES (AP)—Investigators are looking at 30 unsolved murder cases for possible links to a serial killer thought to have claimed at least 11 victims in South Los Angeles.

Detective Dennis Kilcoyne says he believes at least six of those old cases will eventually be tied to the unknown killer, making the case the biggest of its kind ever seen in the city.

Police held a news conference to publicize a city-funded reward of up to $500,000.

The murderer apparently operated in two distinct periods, first from 1985 to 1987, when he killed seven women and a man. He is known to have killed again three times since 2002.

Many victims' bodies were dumped near the same street in South Los Angeles.

Police have a DNA sample of the killer but have been unable to find a match in any prison database.

5. Visit the news department of a local television station. Ask if you can tag along with a crew that is sent out to cover a story. Write 150 words about your experience.

6. Watch an evening television newscast, or listen to a radio news program. Then check the reporting of the same news on the station's website. For each television story reported, write 150 words evaluating how the commentary and video complemented each other on the newscast and how effectively the video was carried over to the Web. For each radio story, write 150 words on how the website story differed from the radio story.

7. Get a copy of today's local newspaper, or consult the paper's website. Write a five-minute radio news broadcast for your area. Devote one minute of the time to sports.

8. **CHALLENGE EXERCISE**

Interview a television news writer about the differences between writing for television and writing for print or the Web. Write 300 words about your interview, focusing on how it complements or contradicts what you read in Chapter 9 in your text.

9. CHALLENGE EXERCISE

Using the following facts, first write a story for print, then for radio/television and then for the Web. Be prepared to explain how the stories differ.

- The quarterback for your school's football team, Brian O'Neil, 20, has been arrested for leaving the scene of an accident.
- Time: Tuesday (yesterday), 1 a.m.
- Place: 26 N. 9th St.
- Police Dept. Spokeswoman Betty Bornokowski said police found O'Neil attempting to flee the scene without notifying the vehicle's owner.
- No one injured.
- O'Neil could face a felony charge if the damage to the car is assessed at more than $1,000.
- O'Neil was released after posting bail, which was set at $5,000.
- No word yet about any possible suspension of O'Neil from football coach Harry Winkle or the school's athletic department.
- O'Neil took over the quarterback position in spring practices when starter Franklin James injured his throwing arm.

Writing for Public Relations

10

1. Comment on this statement: "People working in public relations are journalists in every sense of the word." If you have a journalism blog, post your response on the blog and invite comments from your classmates.

2. What steps would you take in applying for a job in public relations with an association? Write at least 300 words on the subject.

3. A film on YouTube shows the sole attendant at a rental car agency in the Fort Lauderdale Airport walking away from a long line of people waiting to rent a car. What are the first steps you would take to counteract this bad publicity? Write at least 300 words, being as specific as you can about what you would do.

4. Read the following news release. Correct any deviations from Associated Press style and any other errors.

As Grant Elementary School's Partner in Education (PIE), Boone County National Bank is not only giving books to every classroom to celebrate National Children's Book Week, it's also backing up that gift with over fifteen hours of volunteer time. Over 25 bankers will show Grant students they know a lot more than numbers November 15–19 by reading those books to students.

"Our goal is to demonstrate how important reading is to their future success," says Richard Vinhais, Boone County National Bank's PIE Coordinator. "What better way to show our support than to give of ourselves."

The Bank on Books program began as a way for the bank to become involved in Grant's effort to reach its goal of one million reading minutes in one year. This year's goal has stretched to 2.5 million minutes of reading by the school year's end. Rather than just include volunteers in the reading program, the PIE Steering Committee decided it would be great to see professionals taking the time to support the importance of reading.

In addition, the Bank on Books program has become part of Boone County National Bank's commitment to America's Promise. The America's Promise program, initiated by American Bankers Association, serves as a nationwide catalyst, urging public, private and non-profit organizations to focus their combined talents and resources to improve the lives of our nation's youth. The goal is to increase participation by 10 percent in programs directed toward children, a goal easily reached by Boone County National Bank employees.

"As usual, Boone County National Bank people have come through. As busy as the workday is, people were willing to make time for the kids. It's such an important message for them to hear," Vinhais added. Grant Elementary School and Boone County National Bank were two of the founding partners of the Partners in Education Program in 1984. Over the past fifteen years, the

partnership has won 3 national awards for its innovative programs. For more

information about Bank on Books, contact Richard Vinhais at 573-816-8542.

5. Write a news release from the following information. If possible, format the release for a Web page. After you are finished, write a few sentences about which version readers would prefer to read, the one presented here or the one you wrote.

NEWS from CPSC
U.S. Consumer Product Safety Commission

Office of Information and Public Affairs	Washington, DC 20207

FOR IMMEDIATE RELEASE	**Firm's Recall Hotline: (800) 603-9601**
November 26, 2008	CPSC Recall Hotline: (800) 638-2772
Release #09-057	CPSC Media Contact: (301) 504-7908

Stainless Steel Pots Recalled by Ocean State Jobbers
Due to Burn Hazard

WASHINGTON, D.C.—The U.S. Consumer Product Safety Commission, in cooperation with the firm named below, today announced a voluntary recall of the following consumer product. Consumers should stop using recalled products immediately unless otherwise instructed.

Name of Product: Century Cookware Stainless Steel Stockpots

Units: About 7,000

Importer: Ocean State Jobbers Inc., of North Kingstown, R.I.

Hazard: The stainless steel pots have metal handles that can detach during use, posing a serious burn hazard to consumers.

Incidents/Injuries: Ocean State Jobbers has received one report of the handles breaking off a pot and causing a burn injury.

Description: This recall involves the 8-quart, 12-quart, 16-quart, and 20-quart Century Cookware Stainless Steel Stockpots with glass lids. "Century Cookware" is marked on the front and on the bottom of each pot.

Sold at: All Ocean State Job Lot stores throughout New England from July 2008 through October 2008 for between $12 and $25.

Manufactured in: India

Remedy: Consumers should immediately stop using the stockpots and return them to the place of purchase for a full refund.

Consumer Contact: For additional information, contact Ocean State Jobbers at (800) 603-9601 between 8:30 a.m. and 5 p.m. ET Monday through Friday or visit the firm's Web site at www.oceanstatejoblot.com (pdf).

6. Read the following news release carefully. If you were asked to rewrite it for a general audience, what words would you turn into Web links to definitions to help readers understand this article? Circle or highlight the words.

Colorado-based QEP Field Services Agrees to Pay $4 Million and Install Pollution Controls to Resolve Alleged Violations of the Clean Air Act

Release Date: 05/16/2012
Contact Information: Enesta Jones, Jones.enesta@epa.gov, 202-564-7873, 202-564-4355; Stacy Kika, kika.stacy@epa.gov, 202-564-0906, 202-564-4355

WASHINGTON—The U.S. Environmental Protection Agency (EPA) and the U.S. Department of Justice announced a settlement with QEP Field Services Co. (QEPFS), formerly Questar Gas Management Co., to resolve alleged violations of the Clean Air Act at five natural gas compressor stations on the Uintah and Ouray Reservation in Northeastern Utah. Four members of the Ute Indian Tribe intervened as co-plaintiffs. Under the proposed settlement, QEPFS will pay a $3.65 million civil penalty and pay $350,000 into a Clean Air Trust Fund to be established by the tribal member intervenors. The settlement also requires QEPFS to reduce its emissions by removing certain equipment, installing additional pollution controls, and replacing the natural gas powered instrument control systems with compressed air control systems.

"Natural gas extraction projects help to fuel our economy, but also need to follow the nation's laws," said Cynthia Giles, assistant administrator of EPA's Office of Enforcement and Compliance Assurance. "Today's settlement will bring cleaner air to the members of the Northern Ute Tribe by ensuring natural gas compressor stations are operated in compliance with the law and by creating a trust to fund environmental projects on the Uintah and Ouray Reservation."

"This settlement will result in cleaner air for residents living on the Uintah and Ouray reservation and allow the responsible development of energy resources in accordance with the Clean Air Act," said Ignacia S. Moreno, assistant attorney general for the Environment and Natural Resources Division of the Department of Justice. "It also will establish the Tribal Clean Air Trust Fund to fund environmental projects for the benefit of tribal members."

QEPFS's compressor stations remove water and compress natural gas for transportation through gas pipelines. They are sources of air pollution, emitting hazardous air pollutants (HAPs), volatile organic compounds (VOCs), and nitrogen oxides (NO_x), which can increase the risk of asthma attacks and are significant contributors to the formation of ozone. The actions required in the settlement will eliminate approximately 210 tons of NO_x, 219 tons of carbon monoxide, 17 tons of HAPs, and more than 166 tons of VOCs per year. It will also conserve 3.5 million cubic feet of gas each year, which could heat approximately 50 U.S. households. The reduction in methane emissions (a greenhouse gas that is a component of natural gas) is equivalent to planting more than 300 acres of trees.

QEPFS is a wholly-owned subsidiary of QEP Resources, Inc., which is headquartered in Denver. QEPFS provides midstream field services such as natural gas gathering, compression, dehydration and processing to upstream natural gas companies.

The consent decree is subject to a 30-day public comment period and final court approval.

More information about the settlement: http://www.epa.gov/compliance /resources/cases/civil/caa/qepfs.html

7. Read the following news release. First, rewrite the lead. Then create a useful box with information readers can print out and save to remember to go to this event.

First Public Screening of Documentary About History of Missouri Newspapers Set for December 11 in Columbia

The first public screening of "Trustees for the Public: 200 Years of Missouri Newspapers" is scheduled for **Thursday, December 11**, at the Reynolds Journalism Institute at the University of Missouri in Columbia.

A reception in the Reynolds Journalism Institute foyer begins at 5:30 p.m., and the public screening, benefiting Missouri journalism internships, is at 6:30 p.m.

The hour-long documentary celebrates the rich two-century history of Missouri newspapers and the colorful figures associated with them, including Ernest Hemingway, Mark Twain and Joseph Pulitzer, as well as interviews with many contemporary newspaper people from across Missouri and perspectives about the challenges and joys of community newspapering. Produced by the Missouri Press Association, "Trustees for the Public" is scheduled to air this winter on Missouri PBS television stations.

Cost for the December 11 reception and screening is $25 for everyone except students, who will get in free. Proceeds from the screening will be used to fund summer internships at Missouri newspapers for college journalism students.

Each person who buys a ticket to the screening will receive a copy of the one-hour video. Additional copies of the video will be available for $15 each. To purchase tickets for the screening, or to order a copy of the video, contact the Missouri Press Foundation, 802 Locust St., Columbia, MO 65201, or call (573) 449-4167, or e-mail Kristie Williams at kwilliams@socket.net, and the video may be ordered from the MPA site at www.mopress.com.

8. Read this release. Rewrite it to make it more coherent and readable. Also, be sure to emphasize the information you want readers to have.

For more information, contact:
Mark Derowitsch, 888-448-7337 mderowitsch@arborday.org

FOR IMMEDIATE RELEASE

In the Wake of a Storm
What We Can Do to Care for Our Trees After a Storm Hits

Note to the Editor: To help communities with important and practical information about safety and tree care in the wake of a storm, the Arbor Day Foundation has developed free online resources for the media. The Storm Recovery Kit may be reviewed and downloaded for reproduction at arborday.org. The kit includes new information about safety, saving trees, identifying whether a tree can be saved, cutting and pruning, and avoiding scam artists in the wake of a storm.

Nebraska City, Neb.—A major storm can have devastating effects, changing our community in an instant. Buildings may be damaged or destroyed, power lines down, and trees broken and torn. In the wake of this loss, neighborhoods and an entire community may experience a sense of devastation not known before.

"Because trees are such a large part of a city's visual landscape, damage to them from a severe storm can be a major shock to residents," said John

Rosenow, chief executive of the Arbor Day Foundation, an organization that helps people plant and care for trees. "Seeing a favorite tree down or badly damaged in the front yard can be a traumatic experience, almost like losing an old friend."

But Rosenow also said that trees are amazingly resilient and that many recover with proper care.

Information is available from the Arbor Day Foundation for residents who want to become more informed about tree care and storm recovery. The Arbor Day Foundation's Web site, arborday.org, offers a free Storm Recovery Kit, an online set of easy-to-understand guidelines to explain how to care for trees following a severe storm.

Residents will learn to know whether a tree can be saved, the best way to remove broken limbs, and how to identify scam artists posing as arborists.

After a major storm, city officials, utility workers, and private tree care firms have their work cut out for them. The best thing residents can do is be patient and lend a hand.

Citizens can help expedite the city's recovery process by quickly learning correct tree care practices, taking care of simple tasks, and protecting against tree service imposters. For a free Storm Recovery Kit, go to arborday.org.

About the Arbor Day Foundation: The Arbor Day Foundation is a nonprofit conservation organization of nearly one million members, with a mission to inspire people to plant, nurture, and celebrate trees. More information on the Foundation and its programs can be found at arborday.org.

9. Interview a public relations professional. Ask how a media campaign either averted a disaster or helped cope with one. Write a brief report, including a description of how the campaign was conducted.

10. **CHALLENGE EXERCISE**
Look at the calendar of upcoming events at your school. Select an event, contact all of the people involved, and write a news release about it for your local newspaper. Format the release as an email or email attachment, if possible. Then rewrite the release for a local radio station.

Covering a Beat

11

1. Examine the website of your campus or local newspaper, or read its last several print issues. Now answer these questions:
   a. Does the paper have reporters assigned to beats? If so, what are the beats?
   b. Does the same reporter cover a beat for both the print and online editions?
   c. Who are the most-quoted sources? Why?
   d. Do the reporters rely on officials for their stories, or do you see unofficial sources?
   e. For whom do the stories seem to be written: the sources or the readers?
   f. What's your assessment of the overall quality of the paper?

2. From Exercise 1, identify a beat reporter. Arrange to tag along for an afternoon. Play close attention to how she or he cultivates sources and how story ideas become actual stories. Who sets the news agenda: the reporter or the sources? What have you learned from this experience?

3. You've just joined the staff of your campus media. Your first reporting assignment is to cover the central administration. The assigning editor asks how you'll carry out this important responsibility. Reply in a memo.
   a. What sources will be most important?
   b. How will you go about earning the confidence of these sources?
   c. What will be the topic of your first story? Why?

4. You're a consumer of higher education, but do you know what the important issues are that make news? Read the *Chronicle of Higher Education* or other sources, pick a national issue and plan a local story. Your instructor may want a background memo or the story itself.

5. As Chapter 11 points out, the police beat offers great opportunity for good stories but also holds plenty of perils. Assume you've been assigned to cover the police in your city. Write two or three paragraphs explaining how you could avoid the pitfalls while seizing the opportunities.

6. Acknowledging your success in covering the police, your editor asks you to take on the local court system beat, which is closely related. Unlike other beats, however, this assignment doesn't offer regular meetings or officials' offices to cover. Answer the following questions in a memo to your boss:
   a. How will you prepare for this beat?
   b. Who are the most likely sources in your town?
   c. Which websites and online databases might be useful to you?
   d. Which three publications will you find most helpful?

7. As a city hall reporter, you receive the following email press release:

   Mayor Juanita Williams announced today that the city and the Downtown Merchants Association have hired a consulting firm from Washington, D.C., to devise a master plan for redevelopment of the city's central business district. The cost of the plan, estimated at $200,000, will be borne by the city. Mayor Williams said the firm, DHR Inc., was chosen over five other applicants, despite its slightly higher bid, because "the chemistry seems right to us." Mayor Williams said that as a Realtor and downtown businesswoman herself, she knows that the benefit to the city from increased property taxes and revitalized business will return the consultants' fee "10,000 times over." Williams also announced that she would meet with opponents who claim mistakenly that the taxpayers are subsidizing downtown merchants by the city's picking up the whole cost of the study.

   a. Describe the reporting you will need to do in order to write a complete story on the subject of the press release.

   b. How will you keep your readers abreast of the project's developments after that original story?

8. Describe three stories about the police that could be done in your area of the country. What sources would you use for each?

9. Do the same for three possible stories about science, medicine or the environment. Include documentary as well as human sources.

10. Your instructor will assign one of the stories you described in Exercise 8 or 9 and give you a deadline. Report and write the story.

11. Who is your favorite sports writer? Take a close look at her or his work. What makes it so good? How has this writer applied the lessons of this chapter?

12. Check out the message boards and blogs related to your local sports teams or your favorite pro team. How does that content compare with the journalism you've been analyzing? Are message boards and blogs journalism?

13. You've been assigned to cover high school sports for your local newspaper or television station.
    a. Where will you begin your preparation?
    b. What sources will be most useful?

14. Take a close look at local coverage—print, television and radio, and online—of high school sports. How do the media compare? Which do you find most interesting, and why?

15. You have been assigned to cover your college's women's volleyball team. Write a memo describing likely sources and listing three story ideas.

16. You have been assigned to cover your college's track and field program. Write a memo describing likely sources and outlining three story ideas.

17. Describe and list sources for five possible stories on participant sports in your community. The following example shows you what can be done with an event that seldom rates any coverage.

"Break Up Don Johnson."

So went the good-natured battle cry of mere competitors at the Senior Olympics yesterday.

"We're all in shape; we all run and exercise—but did you see the guy who beat me in the mile (run)?" said Jean Madden, who after 57 years still gets wide-eyed after seeing some things. "That guy Johnson is a machine. He's an animal. Did you see him? Unbelievable."

On first approach, Madden's friend, Don Johnson, looked every one of his 55 years. He is a lean 5 ft. 11. His head is having a special on pepper-gray hair these days, and the supply is quickly running out. A thicker forest of steel wool covers his chest. Yesterday, that chest was a heaving rain forest, thoroughly matted down by events.

In the last 12 years, it's been matted down often. It's been drenched by 24 marathons, soaked by three triathlons and rinsed by a sundry of other races. Human Races, Hospital Hill races, Pepsi runs, late-night runs, then sunrise runs. Every week the chest is dampened by 50 to 70 miles of running, 40 miles of bicycling and 54 holes of golf. Some tennis, too.

"I guess I'm what some people would call a fitness freak," Johnson said.

Nah, animal's better. Yesterday morning saw the animal pedaling down Route B from his home in Centralia to Hickman High for the games' opening ceremonies and on to Cosmo Park. The 30-mile ride took him about 90 minutes, but he made it with time to spare before his first event of the day: a 1.6-mile bike race. He won it easily, hopped back on his 10-speed and headed back to Hickman, where he was entered in the mile run. He made the rest of the field look like a slow motion replay, winning in 5 minutes, 31 seconds. He finished second in the 100-meter run, behind Madden. He went to McDonald's for a quick lunch, and then he was headed home on Route B.

Let us try to return Johnson to the planet Earth. Oh, here's something. Friday, he took the family station wagon instead of his bike from Centralia to the L.A. Nickell course at Cosmo, site of the games' golf competition. Animal? He was an old softie.

Old softie got out of that car at Nickell to shoot a 36 to win the golf competition. Animal.

18. CHALLENGE EXERCISE

Often the most useful stories a beat reporter writes are done in advance of meetings at which important issues will be decided. Such advance stories permit readers to take part in the decision-making process, if they so desire. Then, of course, you'll describe the outcome in a story after the meeting. And you may also decide to tweet important news directly from the meeting. Find in your local newspaper or news site both an advance story about a meeting and the story about the actual meeting. Using them as models, prepare for and cover an issue before your school board or city council.

19. CHALLENGE EXERCISE

Your instructor will pick an idea from among those you compiled in response to Exercises 15 to 17. Report and write the story.

Speeches, News Conferences and Meetings

1. What is the value of covering speeches in the age of YouTube, when people can see the speech for themselves whenever they want? Write a one-page report expressing your ideas.

2. Elizabeth Alexander is coming to town to read and discuss her poetry. Prepare to cover the event. List the sources you would consult to learn about Alexander. Then write down in note form what you have gathered from those sources that would be useful in covering the event.

3. The secretary of education is holding a news conference before a meeting of local teachers and school administrators. The secretary is to discuss his views on improving high school graduation rates. List the sources you would consult to prepare for this news conference. Then write down in note form what you have gathered from those sources that would be useful in covering the news conference.

4. Find out when your city council is holding its next meeting. List the sources you would consult to prepare for this meeting. Then write down in note form what you have gathered from those sources that would be useful in covering the meeting.

5. a. Find a story about a speech in a print or online newspaper. Look to see whether the reporter covered both the event itself and the content of the speech. Then analyze the story and comment on the lead, the transitions, the use of quotations and the comprehensiveness of the coverage. Write 300 words.
   b. Do the same for a story about a news conference.
   c. Do the same for a story about a meeting.

6. On wire services or websites, find three stories by three different authors covering a speech or a press conference by the president of the U.S. Compare and analyze the stories. Write 200 words about your findings.

63

7. Write a story covering the content of the following speech.

Remarks in Recognition of International Human Rights Day

Hillary Rodham Clinton, *U.S. Secretary of State*
Delivered at Palais des Nations, Geneva

Good evening, and let me express my deep honor and pleasure at being here. I want to thank Director General Tokayev and Ms. Wyden along with other ministers, ambassadors, excellencies, and UN partners. This weekend, we will celebrate Human Rights Day, the anniversary of one of the great accomplishments of the last century.

Beginning in 1947, delegates from six continents devoted themselves to drafting a declaration that would enshrine the fundamental rights and freedoms of people everywhere. In the aftermath of World War II, many nations pressed for a statement of this kind to help ensure that we would prevent future atrocities and protect the inherent humanity and dignity of all people. And so the delegates went to work. They discussed, they wrote, they revisited, revised, rewrote, for thousands of hours. And they incorporated suggestions and revisions from governments, organizations, and individuals around the world.

At three o'clock in the morning on December 10th, 1948, after nearly two years of drafting and one last long night of debate, the president of the UN General Assembly called for a vote on the final text. Forty-eight nations voted in favor; eight abstained; none dissented. And the Universal Declaration of Human Rights was adopted. It proclaims a simple, powerful idea: All human beings are born free and equal in dignity and rights. And with the declaration, it was made clear that rights are not conferred by government; they are the birthright of all people. It does not matter what country we live in, who our leaders are, or even who we are. Because we are human, we therefore have rights. And because we have rights, governments are bound to protect them.

In the 63 years since the declaration was adopted, many nations have made great progress in making human rights a human reality. Step by step, barriers that once prevented people from enjoying the full measure of liberty, the full experience of dignity, and the full benefits of humanity have fallen away. In many places, racist laws have been repealed, legal and social practices that relegated women to second-class status have been abolished, the ability of religious minorities to practice their faith freely has been secured.

In most cases, this progress was not easily won. People fought and organized and campaigned in public squares and private spaces to change not only laws, but hearts and minds. And thanks to that work of generations, for millions of individuals whose lives were once narrowed by injustice, they are now able to live more freely and to participate more fully in the political, economic, and social lives of their communities.

Now, there is still, as you all know, much more to be done to secure that commitment, that reality, and progress for all people. Today, I want to talk about the work we have left to do to protect one group of people whose human rights are still denied in too many parts of the world today. In many ways, they are an invisible minority. They are arrested, beaten, terrorized, even executed. Many are treated with contempt and violence by their fellow citizens while authorities empowered to protect them look the other way or, too often, even join in the abuse. They are denied opportunities to work and learn, driven from their homes and countries, and forced to suppress or deny who they are to protect themselves from harm.

I am talking about gay, lesbian, bisexual, and transgender people, human beings born free and given bestowed equality and dignity, who have a right to claim that, which is now one of the remaining human rights challenges of our time. I speak about this subject knowing that my own country's record on human rights for gay people is far from perfect. Until 2003, it was still a crime in parts of our country. Many LGBT Americans have endured violence and harassment in their own lives, and for some, including many young people, bullying and exclusion are daily experiences. So we, like all nations, have more work to do to protect human rights at home.

Now, raising this issue, I know, is sensitive for many people and that the obstacles standing in the way of protecting the human rights of LGBT people rest on deeply held personal, political, cultural, and religious beliefs. So I come here before you with respect, understanding, and humility. Even though progress on this front is not easy, we cannot delay acting. So in that spirit, I want to talk about the difficult and important issues we must address together to reach a global consensus that recognizes the human rights of LGBT citizens everywhere.

The first issue goes to the heart of the matter. Some have suggested that gay rights and human rights are separate and distinct; but, in fact, they are one and the same. Now, of course, 60 years ago, the governments that drafted and passed the Universal Declaration of Human Rights were not thinking about how it applied to the LGBT community. They also weren't thinking about how it applied to indigenous people or children or people with disabilities or other marginalized groups. Yet in the past 60 years, we have come to recognize that members of these groups are entitled to the full measure of dignity and rights, because, like all people, they share a common humanity.

This recognition did not occur all at once. It evolved over time. And as it did, we understood that we were honoring rights that people always had, rather than creating new or special rights for them. Like being a woman, like being a racial, religious, tribal, or ethnic minority, being LGBT does not make you less human. And that is why gay rights are human rights, and human rights are gay rights.

It is [a] violation of human rights when people are beaten or killed because of their sexual orientation, or because they do not conform to cultural norms about how men and women should look or behave. It is a violation of human rights when governments declare it illegal to be gay, or allow those who harm gay people to go unpunished. It is a violation of human rights when lesbian or transgendered women are subjected to so-called corrective rape, or forcibly subjected to hormone treatments, or when people are murdered after public calls for violence toward gays, or when they are forced to flee their nations and seek asylum in other lands to save their lives. And it is a violation of human rights when life-saving care is withheld from people because they are gay, or equal access to justice is denied to people because they are gay, or public spaces are out of bounds to people because they are gay. No matter what we look like, where we come from, or who we are, we are all equally entitled to our human rights and dignity.

The second issue is a question of whether homosexuality arises from a particular part of the world. Some seem to believe it is a Western phenomenon, and therefore people outside the West have grounds to reject it. Well, in reality, gay people are born into and belong to every society in the world. They are all ages, all races, all faiths; they are doctors and teachers, farmers and bankers, soldiers and athletes; and whether we know it, or whether we acknowledge it, they are our family, our friends, and our neighbors.

Being gay is not a Western invention; it is a human reality. And protecting the human rights of all people, gay or straight, is not something that only Western governments do. South Africa's constitution, written in the aftermath of Apartheid, protects the equality of all citizens, including gay people. In Colombia and Argentina, the rights of gays are also legally protected. In Nepal, the supreme court has ruled that equal rights apply to LGBT citizens. The Government of Mongolia has committed to pursue new legislation that will tackle anti-gay discrimination.

Now, some worry that protecting the human rights of the LGBT community is a luxury that only wealthy nations can afford. But in fact, in all countries, there are costs to not protecting these rights, in both gay and straight lives lost to disease and violence, and the silencing of voices and views that would strengthen communities, in ideas never pursued by entrepreneurs who happen to be gay. Costs are incurred whenever any group is treated as lesser or the other, whether they are women, racial, or religious minorities, or the LGBT. Former President Mogae of Botswana pointed out recently that for as long as LGBT people are kept in the shadows, there cannot be an effective public health program to tackle HIV and AIDS. Well, that holds true for other challenges as well.

The third, and perhaps most challenging, issue arises when people cite religious or cultural values as a reason to violate or not to protect the human rights of LGBT citizens. This is not unlike the justification offered for violent practices towards women like honor killings, widow burning, or female genital mutilation. Some people still defend those practices as part of a cultural tradition. But violence toward women isn't cultural; it's criminal. Likewise with slavery, what was once justified as sanctioned by God is now properly reviled as an unconscionable violation of human rights.

In each of these cases, we came to learn that no practice or tradition trumps the human rights that belong to all of us. And this holds true for inflicting violence on LGBT people, criminalizing their status or behavior, expelling them from their families and communities, or tacitly or explicitly accepting their killing.

Of course, it bears noting that rarely are cultural and religious traditions and teachings actually in conflict with the protection of human rights. Indeed, our religion and our culture are sources of compassion and inspiration toward our fellow human beings. It was not only those who've justified slavery who leaned on religion, it was also those who sought to abolish it. And let us keep in mind that our commitments to protect the freedom of religion and to defend the dignity of LGBT people emanate from a common source. For many of us, religious belief and practice is a vital source of meaning and identity, and fundamental to who we are as people. And likewise, for most of us, the bonds of love and family that we forge are also vital sources of meaning and identity. And caring for others is an expression of what it means to be fully human. It is because the human experience is universal that human rights are universal and cut across all religions and cultures.

The fourth issue is what history teaches us about how we make progress towards rights for all. Progress starts with honest discussion. Now, there are some who say and believe that all gay people are pedophiles, that homosexuality is a disease that can be caught or cured, or that gays recruit others to become gay. Well, these notions are simply not true. They are also unlikely to disappear if those who promote or accept them are dismissed out of hand rather than invited to share their fears and concerns. No one has ever abandoned a belief because he was forced to do so.

Universal human rights include freedom of expression and freedom of belief, even if our words or beliefs denigrate the humanity of others. Yet, while we are each free to believe whatever we choose, we cannot do whatever we choose, not in a world where we protect the human rights of all.

Reaching understanding of these issues takes more than speech. It does take a conversation. In fact, it takes a constellation of conversations in places big and small. And it takes a willingness to see stark differences in belief as a reason to begin the conversation, not to avoid it.

But progress comes from changes in laws. In many places, including my own country, legal protections have preceded, not followed, broader recognition of rights. Laws have a teaching effect. Laws that discriminate validate other kinds of discrimination. Laws that require equal protections reinforce the moral imperative of equality. And practically speaking, it is often the case that laws must change before fears about change dissipate.

Many in my country thought that President Truman was making a grave error when he ordered the racial desegregation of our military. They argued that it would undermine unit cohesion. And it wasn't until he went ahead and did it that we saw how it strengthened our social fabric in ways even the supporters of the policy could not foresee. Likewise, some worried in my country that the repeal of "Don't Ask, Don't Tell" would have a negative effect on our armed forces. Now, the Marine Corps Commandant, who was one of the strongest voices against the repeal, says that his concerns were unfounded and that the Marines have embraced the change.

Finally, progress comes from being willing to walk a mile in someone else's shoes. We need to ask ourselves, "How would it feel if it were a crime to love the person I love? How would it feel to be discriminated against for something about myself that I cannot change?" This challenge applies to all of us as we reflect upon deeply held beliefs, as we work to embrace tolerance and respect for the dignity of all persons, and as we engage humbly with those with whom we disagree in the hope of creating greater understanding.

A fifth and final question is how we do our part to bring the world to embrace human rights for all people including LGBT people. Yes, LGBT people must help lead this effort, as so many of you are. Their knowledge and experiences are invaluable and their courage inspirational. We know the names of brave LGBT activists who have literally given their lives for this cause, and there are many more whose names we will never know. But often those who are denied rights are least empowered to bring about the changes they seek. Acting alone, minorities can never achieve the majorities necessary for political change.

So when any part of humanity is sidelined, the rest of us cannot sit on the sidelines. Every time a barrier to progress has fallen, it has taken a cooperative effort from those on both sides of the barrier. In the fight for women's rights, the support of men remains crucial. The fight for racial equality has relied on contributions from people of all races. Combating Islamaphobia or anti-Semitism is a task for people of all faiths. And the same is true with this struggle for equality.

Conversely, when we see denials and abuses of human rights and fail to act, that sends the message to those deniers and abusers that they won't suffer any consequences for their actions, and so they carry on. But when we do act, we send a powerful moral message. Right here in Geneva, the international community acted this year to strengthen a global consensus around the human rights of LGBT people. At the Human Rights Council in March, 85 countries from all regions supported a statement calling for an end to criminalization and violence against people because of their sexual orientation and gender identity.

At the following session of the Council in June, South Africa took the lead on a resolution about violence against LGBT people. The delegation from South Africa spoke eloquently about their own experience and struggle for human equality and its indivisibility. When the measure passed, it became the first-ever UN resolution recognizing the human rights of gay people worldwide. In the Organization of American States this year, the Inter-American Commission on Human Rights created a unit on the rights of LGBT people, a step toward what we hope will be the creation of a special rapporteur.

Now, we must go further and work here and in every region of the world to galvanize more support for the human rights of the LGBT community. To the leaders of those countries where people are jailed, beaten, or executed for being gay, I ask you to consider this: Leadership, by definition, means being out in front of your people when it is called for. It means standing up for the dignity of all your citizens and persuading your people to do the same. It also means ensuring that all citizens are treated as equals under your laws, because let me be clear—I am not saying that gay people can't or don't commit crimes. They can and they do, just like straight people. And when they do, they should be held accountable, but it should never be a crime to be gay.

And to people of all nations, I say supporting human rights is your responsibility too. The lives of gay people are shaped not only by laws, but by the treatment they receive every day from their families, from their neighbors. Eleanor Roosevelt, who did so much to advance human rights worldwide, said that these rights begin in the small places close to home—the streets where people live, the schools they attend, the factories, farms, and offices where they work. These places are your domain. The actions you take, the ideals that you advocate, can determine whether human rights flourish where you are.

And finally, to LGBT men and women worldwide, let me say this: Wherever you live and whatever the circumstances of your life, whether you are connected to a network of support or feel isolated and vulnerable, please know that you are not alone. People around the globe are working hard to support you and to bring an end to the injustices and dangers you face. That is certainly true for my country. And you have an ally in the United States of America and you have millions of friends among the American people.

The Obama Administration defends the human rights of LGBT people as part of our comprehensive human rights policy and as a priority of our foreign policy. In our embassies, our diplomats are raising concerns about specific cases and laws, and working with a range of partners to strengthen human rights protections for all. In Washington, we have created a task force at the State Department to support and coordinate this work. And in the coming months, we will provide every embassy with a toolkit to help improve their efforts. And we have created a program that offers emergency support to defenders of human rights for LGBT people.

This morning, back in Washington, President Obama put into place the first U.S. Government strategy dedicated to combating human rights abuses against LGBT persons abroad. Building on efforts already underway at the State Department and across the government, the President has directed all U.S. Government agencies engaged overseas to combat the criminalization of LGBT status and conduct, to enhance efforts to protect vulnerable LGBT refugees and asylum seekers, to ensure that our foreign assistance promotes the protection of LGBT rights, to enlist international organizations in the fight against discrimination, and to respond swiftly to abuses against LGBT persons.

I am also pleased to announce that we are launching a new Global Equality Fund that will support the work of civil society organizations working on these issues around the world. This fund will help them record facts so they can target their advocacy, learn how to use the law as a tool, manage their budgets, train their staffs, and forge partnerships with women's organizations and other human rights groups. We have committed more than $3 million to start this fund, and we have hope that others will join us in supporting it.

The women and men who advocate for human rights for the LGBT community in hostile places, some of whom are here today with us, are brave and dedicated, and deserve all the help we can give them. We know the road ahead will not be easy. A great deal of work lies before us. But many of us have seen first-hand how quickly change can come. In our lifetimes, attitudes toward gay people in many places have been transformed. Many people, including myself, have experienced a deepening of our own convictions on this topic over the years, as we have devoted more thought to it, engaged in dialogues and debates, and established personal and professional relationships with people who are gay.

This evolution is evident in many places. To highlight one example, the Delhi High Court decriminalized homosexuality in India two years ago, writing, and I quote, "If there is one tenet that can be said to be an underlying theme of the Indian constitution, it is inclusiveness." There is little doubt in my mind that support for LGBT human rights will continue to climb. Because for many young people, this is simple: All people deserve to be treated with dignity and have their human rights respected, no matter who they are or whom they love.

There is a phrase that people in the United States invoke when urging others to support human rights: "Be on the right side of history." The story of the United States is the story of a nation that has repeatedly grappled with intolerance and inequality. We fought a brutal civil war over slavery. People from coast to coast joined in campaigns to recognize the rights of women, indigenous peoples, racial minorities, children, people with disabilities, immigrants, workers, and on and on. And the march toward equality and justice has continued. Those who advocate for expanding the circle of human rights were and are on the right side of history, and history honors them. Those who tried to constrict human rights were wrong, and history reflects that as well.

I know that the thoughts I've shared today involve questions on which opinions are still evolving. As it has happened so many times before, opinion will converge once again with the truth, the immutable truth, that all persons are created free and equal in dignity and rights. We are called once more to make real the words of the Universal Declaration. Let us answer that call. Let us be on the right side of history, for our people, our nations, and future generations, whose lives will be shaped by the work we do today. I come before you with great hope and confidence that no matter how long the road ahead, we will travel it successfully together. Thank you very much.

8. Jessica Jergens, the head of journalism at your school, is holding a press conference to announce that she has resigned from her position. She charges that the school has provided insufficient funding for the journalism program to function properly. Write at least one tweet (140 characters) that you would send during the news conference. Then write a story for your local newspaper covering the content of the news conference. Do not exceed 1,000 words.

Opening Statement

Ladies and gentlemen, I have called this news conference to announce that at the end of this school term, I shall be resigning my position as head of journalism. It has been no secret that I have had some serious differences with the administration of this university over how the journalism program continues to be funded. The faculty in journalism are too few and too poorly paid. The facilities are pathetic by anyone's standards. This university does students no favor by sending them out into the world of journalism improperly prepared. I can no longer in good conscience head a program that has so little support.

When I came on board five years ago, I thought we had an understanding that I could bring on one new person each year for at least five years. In those five years, our faculty has increased by only one. Although we acquired some new equipment, our news writing lab still has manual typewriters.

Although the administration can cite lack of funding generally, it cannot explain how one can run a program successfully without proper support.

Questions and Answers

Q. Dr. Jergens, are you recommending that the journalism program in this university be dropped altogether?

A. I am not saying that. Perhaps my departure will help the administration see the seriousness of the situation and do something to remedy it. I personally think it would be a tremendous loss to the university not to have a journalism program.

Q. Are you merely resigning your position as head of journalism, or are you also leaving the university?

A. I am leaving the university.

Q. Do you have any future plans?

A. Well, I am going to take it easy for at least a year. I have some writing to do and a lot of reading to catch up on.

Q. What is your primary complaint? What didn't you get that made you resign?

A. I thought I made myself clear on that.

Q. But what was the final straw? What made you quit now?

A. Well, I had set certain goals for myself. When I came, I realized the journalism program needed strengthening in many areas. If we were going to be a well-rounded program, we needed courses added. You need qualified faculty to teach courses. It all starts with qualified faculty. I guess I had something of a five-year plan. If I didn't get to a certain point in five years, I thought it would be a pretty good indication that this university was not serious in its commitment to a quality journalism program.

Q. If the situation is so bad, how do you expect the university to recruit a new head? Who would take this job?

A. Hope springs eternal. There's always someone out there who would like to have a shot at this.

Q. Is there someone on the faculty now whom you would recommend?

A. I am not sure I would wish this job on anyone who knows the situation here well. But if you are asking whether anyone on this faculty is capable and qualified to handle this position, of course there are several. Any of several could succeed—if the administration comes through with more support.

Q. What is your proudest achievement as head of journalism?

A. The curriculum is stronger now than it was five years ago. The faculty is stronger as well. I also believe we have attracted a better brand of student.

Q. Is there any truth to the rumor that lack of cooperation among your faculty is the real reason you are stepping down?

A. That would be news to me. I have had my differences with one or two members of this faculty, but I cannot complain about a lack of faculty support.

Q. What about the rumor that the administration has asked you to step down but gave you a chance to resign?

A. That is altogether incorrect. Perhaps my resignation will cause some joy in the halls of the administration, but no one has asked me to resign or even suggested that I resign.

Q. Dr. Jergens, you are not denying that you have at times engaged in open warfare with the president of this university, are you?

A. I have not been asked that question. All I am saying is that no one has asked me to resign. And that includes the president of this university.

Q. Do you think you have enjoyed wide support among this student body? Hasn't there been a great deal of student dissatisfaction?

A. I will leave that to others to answer. However, you may consult a student survey conducted less than a year ago that indicated that students gave me an above-average rating. You may compare my rating to the heads of other areas that have taken such a survey.

Q. What is your single biggest regret?

A. Well, it has to be that times and people are such that proper funding is simply not forthcoming. Perhaps I and others have failed to impress this university and people in general of the importance of journalism in a free society and how badly we need to train people well.

Q. What one thing would you most wish for the journalism program?

A. Better writing classes. The biggest complaint in any area of professional journalism is that we are not turning out good writers. Writing classes must be taught by qualified faculty, and those classes have to be small enough for the professor to be able to give the kind of attention students need. Everything begins and ends with writing.

Q. Will you return to teaching, or will you seek work in the real world of journalism?

A. I don't think I have ever left the real world of journalism. But yes, I can't imagine that I will leave teaching.

Q. What about another administrative post?

A. For the time being, no, thank you.

9. The mayor of your city, James Alton, holds two news conferences every month. Here's a transcript of one of them. Write a story for your local newspaper on this conference. Do not exceed 1,000 words.

Opening Statement

Ladies and gentlemen, I have no startling announcement today or any shocking news. I am pleased to tell you that local crime is down 9 percent from last year at this time. I believe our efforts to strengthen the police force and to make neighborhoods aware of their responsibilities to combat crime are paying off.

We must all continue working to make the streets of our city safe. That includes safety from traffic accidents. Unfortunately, five more people have been killed in traffic accidents in our city than were killed a year ago.

Not surprisingly, alcohol was involved in four of those fatalities. We will crack down even harder on drunken driving and will continue to push for a tougher ordinance on first- and second-time offenders.

What's on your minds today?

Questions and Answers

Q. Mr. Mayor, what kind of ordinance would you like to see enforced regarding drunken driving?

A. Well, I have been thinking about this for some time now, and it seems to me that first offenders should spend a night in jail and have their licenses revoked for 90 days. Second offenders should spend 30 days in jail and have their licenses revoked for one year. Three or more offenses should carry a mandatory sentence of six months in jail and license revoked for five years.

Q. Don't you think you are being a bit severe, especially with first offenders?

A. No, I don't. Drunken driving kills. If someone drives while intoxicated, that person is a potential killer, a threat to every citizen. That person is similar to someone going around with a loaded, cocked gun. But even the person with the gun might have some control. The drunken driver is out of control.

Q. You speak of sending a lot more people to jail. Where do you propose to put them? Our jail is already too crowded.

A. You're right. We have a serious problem there. The voters of this community have turned down the means to enlarge our jail three years in a row now. Somehow, we have not found the way to get citizens to see how desperate the situation is. The crowded jail is a disgrace to this community. Even more disgraceful is that we have released prisoners only because of lack of space.

Q. Isn't it true also that some have clearly received lighter sentences because of a lack of jail space?

A. I don't want to comment on that. I would have to know of specific examples. Right now I don't have one.

Q. Here's one. The police chief's son was just sentenced to serve six months in jail on three charges of driving with a revoked license and one charge of driving with a suspended license. Don't you think that is a light sentence, and do you think the jail situation has something to do with it?

A. Let me answer the second question first. No, I think the jail situation had nothing to do with the sentencing of that young man . . .

Q. What was it, then, the fact that he is the son of the police chief?

A. Answering your first question is a bit more difficult. Was it a light sentence? If I remember the facts correctly, he was sentenced to serve one year for driving with a revoked license, but that sentence was suspended. Instead he was placed on two years' probation and ordered to perform 40 hours of community service and to pay court costs. He was then given three concurrent six-month terms in jail on three other charges: two counts of driving with a revoked license and one of driving with a suspended license. So he has six months in jail, plus community service.

Q. But surely this sentence does not speak well for improving the safety of drivers and pedestrians in our community. Why haven't you been vocal in urging stronger sentences in cases like these?

A. I don't know that it is my place to second-guess a judge.

Q. Mr. Mayor, do you or do you not think the police chief's son got off too easy?

A. Yes, I do.

Q. Well, which is it?

A. I think the sentence was light.

Q. There has been a blight of school bus accidents around the country. Some have pointed to the young, inexperienced drivers of these school buses. This community has 12 drivers below the age of 20. Three of them are 18. Do you think we should be entrusting the lives of our children to 18-year-old drivers?

A. I am not sure that age has much to do with driving skills. You could argue, I suppose, that experience helps. After all, the jet fighter pilots of our Air Force are often under 20, I'm told. Young people have quicker reflexes, and they can be excellent drivers.

Q. But what excuse can there be to let inexperienced drivers drive our school buses?

A. Money.

Q. You mean we can't pay mature, experienced drivers enough, so we have to hire kids?

A. Of course.

Q. But that's outrageous.

A. Tell the taxpayers that. You have to understand that a bus driver's hours often make it impossible for that person to hold down another job. People with solid, well-paying jobs are not likely to become school bus drivers.

Q. The vice chairman of the Springfield Tomorrow Committee resigned this past week because he was unable "to stand the pettiness of the press." What is your reaction to that?

A. Well, I guess I have known you folks to be petty from time to time. I'm sorry Gerald Nicklaus felt that way. Any public position demands that we put up with you people.

Q. Is that your understanding of the press, that you have to "put up" with us?

A. Of course not. You know that I know that we can't exist without you people.

Q. Let's return to Mr. Nicklaus. You must have known that he ordered a committee selection meeting to be held Tuesday without the public or media present. Did you approve of this order? Or did you ask for his resignation?

A. I neither approved of the action nor asked for his resignation.

Q. Why didn't you ask for his resignation?

A. Well, I would have at least given him a chance to change his mind on the subject. Had he persisted on closed meetings, I don't suppose there was any choice but to ask him to step down.

Q. His letter of resignation also cited poor health. Do you believe that was the reason?

A. I only know what he said, and I have no reason to disbelieve him.

Q. When will you name his replacement?

A. I hope by the end of the week.

Q. Mr. Mayor, what about the rumors that you and Mrs. Alton are living in separate residences?

A. Thank you, ladies and gentlemen.

10. **CHALLENGE EXERCISE**

Using computer databases to search for information, prepare for, cover and write the following:

a. A speech story.

b. A news conference story.

c. A meeting story.

Then for each story, write a paragraph comparing your story with a story on the same event appearing in the local paper.

Writing Common Types of Stories

13

Stories Covering Crime and the Courts

1. In almost any crime story, there are three major sources of information. List those sources, and briefly describe what kind of information you would expect to obtain from each.

2. You are sent to the scene of a bank robbery, where you find that the police and the FBI are still investigating. Describe what steps you would take to get as much information as possible for an early edition of your newspaper or for an imminent television broadcast.

3. Obtain from your campus police department crime statistics for the previous year as reported to the federal government. Using *Crime in the United States*, published annually by the FBI, write a story comparing crime on your campus with overall U.S. figures.

4. Write a story based on the following information obtained from police and other sources:
   a. The Black Derby Liquor Store, 2311 Ripley Way, was robbed at gunpoint.
   b. The clerk was Steve Bellinos of 4673 Bellinghausen Court. His age is 28.
   c. A man with a pillowcase over his head entered the store at 7:12 p.m. He pulled out a pistol and demanded that Bellinos empty the contents of the cash register into another pillowcase.
   d. Police officers Anne Fulgham and Jose Lopez answered a silent alarm triggered by Bellinos at 7:16 p.m. They arrived at the store at 7:19 p.m. as the gunman was leaving the store.
   e. The man fled as he saw the police car. Officer Fulgham shouted a warning and fired a shot at the man, but she missed. The man ran into an alley, and the two officers followed. He finally escaped.
   f. A witness, John Paul Reinicke, 35, of 109 Ninth St., Apt. 3C, was walking down Ripley Way when the incident occurred. "The officers did a great job," he said. "The guy ran so fast he looked like a track star."
   g. The owner of the liquor store, Ralph Martinson, 53, of 109 Lincoln Terrace, said about $2,845 was taken.
   h. Police Chief Antonio Grasso said a routine investigation of the incident would be made by the Police Internal Security Squad. Such investigations are conducted each time an officer fires a service revolver.
   i. The clerk said the robber was about 6 feet tall and weighed 155 pounds. He was wearing blue jeans and a dirty white T-shirt with a torn right sleeve.

5. Write a story based on the following information obtained from police and other sources:
   a. Danielle D. Drummond, 19, of 209 Rodgers Hall on the local campus, was raped.
   b. Location was by the Chemistry Building as Drummond was walking back to her dorm after going to a movie downtown. She was alone.
   c. A man with a stocking mask displayed a knife and forced her into an alley beside the Chemistry Building. He threatened to kill her if she screamed.
   d. She described the man as 6 feet 4 inches tall, 210 pounds, athletic appearance, blond hair, blue eyes, scar on the left side of his neck.
   e. Police said the description was similar to that given by two other victims of rapes in the campus area in the past six months. In all, there have been four rapes in the area during that period.
   f. One of the other victims also said the man wore a stocking mask. In the two other assaults, no mask was used. All involved the use of a knife.
   g. The reported rape is the 16th in the city this year, compared with two during the same period last year.
   h. Police Chief Grasso said he is forming a rape task force composed of police, rape crisis center officials and others to determine what can be done about the series of rapes.
   i. College officials say they will install emergency telephone lines in outdoor areas around the campus and review street lighting in the area.

6. Analyze the following court story, and write a critique of it. Pay particular attention to the flow of the story and the attention to detail. Also, describe how the story might have been improved.

Friends of a murdered man gathered Monday in the Lincoln County Courthouse to hear a life sentence pronounced for Lilah Butler, convicted in February of conspiring to kill her husband.

Judge Linda Garrett denied her motion for a new trial and ordered her to spend her first night behind bars Monday.

Lilah Butler has been free on a $500,000 bond since a jury convicted her of first-degree murder and recommended a life sentence without possibility of parole.

Danny Johnson admitted killing Alfredo Butler but said he did it at Lilah Butler's urging, convinced by her promises of a life together and $200,000 in life insurance money.

The crowd of Alfredo Butler's friends and co-workers stirred and murmured as defense attorney Joel Eisenstein asked Garrett to allow his client to remain free on bond. Even before the murder, they said, Lilah Butler had ruined her husband's life.

"He changed from one day to the other" after his marriage, Heinz Albertson said. Albertson moved from Switzerland in 1981 with Alfredo Butler, but Butler stopped seeing his friends after the marriage, and "his smile disappeared."

Another Swiss friend, Rudi Bieri, described Lilah Butler as a "spoiled brat." He said Alfredo Butler told him that his wife had threatened his life more than once.

"He knew it was coming," said Jane Welliver, a co-worker of the victim. Two weeks before the murder, she said, Alfredo Butler told her that his wife was going to kill him, that she had held him at gunpoint several times, once waking him with a gun at his head. Co-worker Marcus Polzner said he felt relieved at the sentence. "It's long overdue."

The case has also been a tragedy for the family of Lilah Butler, many of whom attended Monday. Her mother broke down as the defendant was turned over to uniformed court officers. Her father is the presiding circuit judge of Dent County, and her uncle is a judge there.

Two brothers, both attorneys, watched as Eisenstein argued for two hours in his attempt to convince the court that Lilah Butler deserved a new trial. He requested a postponement of the sentence so he could gather more evidence that one of the state's most damaging witnesses had perjured himself during the trial.

Eisenstein maintained that the prosecution had a secret deal with Billy Goodwin, who testified that Lilah

Butler told him she wanted to get rid of her husband and she knew how to get away with it because she was trained as a police officer. Lilah Butler had been an officer on the St. Francois police force.

The investigator for the prosecution flatly denied any such deal Monday. The only evidence Eisenstein offered was that an outstanding warrant against Goodwin had been dropped. His motion was denied.

7. Analyze the following story, and write a critique of it. Pay particular attention to the flow of the story and the attention to detail. Also, describe how the story might have been improved.

No lights, no cameras, no action.

Two months after the state Supreme Court's decision to experiment with cameras in some circuit courtrooms, the idea seems to be stalled in the talking stages.

Although the two-year experiment is still in its early stages, only one media request for coverage of a trial has been filed in the 13th Judicial Circuit, which includes Lincoln and Callaway counties, said media coordinator Carlos Fernandez. The state Supreme Court appointed Fernandez to handle all media requests for judicial proceedings in the circuit.

With 46 states already allowing still cameras, audio equipment and video cameras in their courtrooms, this state lags far behind. The conservative makeup of the state Supreme Court might be partly responsible, some observers say. The change of judges within the past few years, however, gave the idea new life, said Roger Cruise, executive director of the state Press Association.

"Cameras in the courtroom have been talked about here for years and years," Cruise said. "But it took a change in the Supreme Court."

Lincoln County Presiding Circuit Judge Robert Wagner agreed: "I think it is just a change in philosophy among the people on the bench," he said. "We have a different court in the state capital."

Courtrooms have been off-limits to electronic media coverage, but the state Supreme Court in October approved the experiment for the high court and the appeals courts. On Jan. 13, the high court announced that some trial courts—including the 13th Judicial Circuit and 10 other circuits—would be part of the experiment. Wagner co-chaired a 17-member statewide task force to investigate and oversee the experiment.

"Assuming that the coverage is done correctly," Wagner said, cameras will allow the public "to better understand what goes on in the courtroom."

Even advocates of the change harbor reservations. "My primary concern is to see to it that the defendant gets a fair trial," Wagner said. "This is not a First Amendment right; it is a Fifth Amendment concern."

Wagner listed potential drawbacks to cameras in the courtroom, especially in areas involving victims of sexual assault. Lincoln County Prosecutor James Taylor agreed that witness testimony is a primary concern.

"I wouldn't want to have a situation where a victim of a crime, who did not want to be publicly identified, was subjected to that," Taylor said.

Part of the experiment, titled Administrative Rule 16, provides for crime victims, police informants, undercover agents, juveniles and relocated witnesses to object to being filmed. The trial judge makes the final decision.

Dzuigas Kramer, a KBCD-TV editor and media coordinator for the 8th Circuit in Boonville, said he previously worked in Florida and California, where cameras in the courtrooms "were just a matter of fact."

The procedure in those states is to contact the judge and fill out a request, both of which can be done the day of the judicial proceeding, Kramer said.

The experiment, in most cases, requires a request 14 days in advance to the media coordinator, who must file with attorneys and the judge at least 10 days before proceedings.

Judges can alter the rules. Television coverage of a Boonville murder trial in February—which would have been the first TV trial in the state—was stymied by restrictions outlined by the judge, Robert Dowler.

After several television stations requested permission to cover the Eaton Fleming case, Dowler ruled that the coverage would be severely limited and that he would preview the videotapes, Kramer said. "Television stations declined under the conditions that the judge stipulated.

"We felt we could not abide by them," he added.

The defense attorneys and the prosecutors in the Fleming case were also opposed to camera coverage, Kramer said.

Cruise said he believes an agreement can be reached between the judges' concerns for a fair trial and journalists' desire to cover it. "The judge has to have some control. On the other hand, if media follow the guidelines set down, they should be able to use the material without review."

The Supreme Court's Task Force on Cameras in the Courtroom is monitoring both the appeals courts' and the trial courts' experiments and will report its findings to the high court at the end of the year. Then the Supreme Court will apply the rule to all state courts permanently, continue the experiment or reinstate the statewide ban on electronic coverage.

8. John R. Wallinger, 29, of 202 Park Place, has been arrested in connection with the robbery in Exercise 4. He was taken to Magistrate Court, where he entered a plea of not guilty. He claims to be indigent, and the judge, Darla Mickelson, appointed Linda Treator as his court-appointed attorney. Write a story about the court appearance.

9. Write a story based on the following information obtained from police and other sources:
   a. John A. Intaglio, 22, of 2909 Richardson St., has been arrested in connection with seven burglaries of homes and businesses during the past year.
   b. The burglaries took place on the following dates at the indicated locations:
      1. Roger's Liquors, 202 Delmore St., $250 in cash, Sept. 8.
      2. Bill Rhone Texaco, 1212 Fifth St., $23 in cash and calculator, Sept. 17.
      3. Linda Poole residence, 2000 Dickerson Ave., $200 in cash and $300 in jewelry, Sept. 20.
      4. Ron Doyle residence, 2180 Dickerson Ave., $2,000 fur coat, Sept. 26.
      5. Denny Doyle residence, 209 Drolling Place, $10 in cash, Nov. 12.
      6. Miller Bros. department store, 209 Main St., $2,800 in merchandise, Feb.
      7. Don and Linda Hopson residence, 333 E. Briarwood St., $20 in cash and coins valued at $2,900, July 19.
   c. Police Chief Antonio Grasso said, "We think this guy could be involved in as many as 40 other burglaries during the past year."
   d. Grasso said investigators started checking on the suspect after he sold some of the stolen items to a well-known fence. The fence has fled town, and a warrant for his arrest has been issued. The warrant is sealed.
   e. Other items were found in the suspect's home to link him to some of the burglaries with which he is charged.
   f. Prosecutor Ralph Gingrich said the suspect will be charged with seven counts of burglary, seven counts of stealing and four counts of selling stolen merchandise. Other charges will be filed as burglary cases involving the suspect are cleared.
   g. Chief Grasso would not comment on whether this suspect may have been involved in an attempted burglary last month in which a 34-year-old woman was shot to death by a burglar.
   h. That incident occurred when Barbara Dueringer was awakened in her room at 3335 Grossman Lane. She screamed, and the man fled and shot her roommate to death on the way out of the house. The roommate was Mary Dillinger.
   i. Recovered items will be returned to the owners after the trial.

10. John A. Intaglio is being tried in Circuit Court on seven counts of burglary, as described in Exercise 9. Using the supplemental information obtained in the courtroom appearance, write a court story:
   a. Intaglio's lawyer is Richard Delano, 2020 First St., a well-known criminal lawyer. He handled the infamous murder case of John D'Aquisto, who was found innocent of murdering First Ward City Councilman Roger Baker last year.
   b. Delano calls for a mistrial on grounds that the judge, Thompson Dickerson III, is prejudiced against Italian-Americans. Intaglio is Italian-American. The judge, Delano claims, has tried 14 cases involving

defendants of Italian descent in the six years he has been on the bench, and all 14 were convicted. The judge dismisses the motion and says, "You would be wise, Mr. Delano, to concentrate on defending your client. Leave the rest to me. I can assure you that I like Italians, and I like pizza, too."

c. Police Detective William O'Shaunessy testifies that the merchandise found in Intaglio's home was positively identified by the owners. He says that Intaglio admitted to stealing the items. Delano objects to the testimony about the confession and requests a mistrial. The motion is denied, but the judge orders the statement stricken from the record and tells the jury to ignore it.

d. The judge adjourns the trial for the day. The jury is dismissed.

11. John A. Intaglio is acquitted. Write a story using the data in Exercises 9 and 10 and the following information:

a. Delano, the defense attorney, says, "Justice has been served. My client has been persecuted by the police, the prosecutor and the judge. A wise jury saw through all that."

b. Prosecutor Gingrich says, "I'm appalled. It all goes to show that sometimes the system doesn't work. I thought our case was airtight. We'll have another chance, though. We plan to try him in connection with some other burglaries. This man (Intaglio) should be off the streets."

c. The jury deliberated only 20 minutes before returning its verdict. None of the jurors would comment.

12. Define the following terms:

a. Preliminary hearing

b. Arraignment

c. Probable cause

d. Change of venue

13. You are assigned to cover a preliminary hearing in a murder case. What information would you expect to obtain at such a hearing?

14. The trial in a major kidnapping case begins tomorrow, and you have been assigned to write a pretrial story. With whom would you talk, and why?

15. Attend a session of traffic court in your city, and write a story based on one of the cases heard. If none is particularly interesting, write a story that describes how the traffic court operates.

16. Attend a criminal trial at your local courthouse, and write a story for your blog based on the testimony there. Check newspaper clippings that reported on the incident at the time to help you develop proper background.

17. Murders in Holyfield, Kan., rose from one in 2010 to seven in 2012, but rapes fell from 35 to 27, robberies from 97 to 86 and assaults from 302 to 280. Meanwhile, burglaries rose from 576 to 603 and larcenies from 3,404 to 3,420. Auto theft remained the same at 172.
a. Write a news story based on these crime statistics.
b. Create a simple chart to accompany your story.

18. List all of the sources the reporter used to write the following story. Also list additional sources that might have improved the story.

The trial date for Angelica Jackson, the Mississippi woman charged in the stabbing death of her boyfriend, has been reset for May 25. Judge Todd B. Schwartz granted the extension to allow the defense more time to conduct investigations.

Jackson, 20, had testified that she stabbed her boyfriend, Mark Thomasson, also from Mississippi, on Dec. 13 while the couple was visiting relatives in Springfield. Jackson said Thomasson accused her of having an incestuous affair with her father. She is charged with second-degree murder, which carries a sentence of 10 years to life.

Associate Public Defender Rahsetnu Miller said Jackson is a victim of battered woman syndrome. Miller has been investigating information on Thomasson's possible criminal record. He hopes to interview about 10 witnesses. "It's my understanding that he (Thomasson) has had some scrapes with the criminal justice system down there," Miller said.

Thomasson was awaiting trial on a drug case before his stabbing death, he said. Miller hopes to find additional evidence that Jackson was abused by an "intoxicated man with a past violent record."

Stories Covering Accidents, Fires and Disasters

19. Your editor has sent you to the local river, where a young girl is believed to have drowned. From whom would you try to obtain information, and what would you expect to get from each of them?

20. You are covering a tornado and would like to include damage estimates in your story. From whom would you obtain those estimates?

21. You are covering a house fire that resulted in the loss of housing for a family of four. You would like to find out what relief help will be forthcoming. From whom would you obtain that information?

22. Write an accident story from the following information extracted from a police accident report:

> VEHICLE NO. 1: Car driven by Kelvin L. Bowen, 16, 513 Maple Lane. Son of Mr. and Mrs. Lawrence K. Bowen. Passenger: Brad Levitt, 16, 208 Maple Lane.
>
> VEHICLE NO. 2: A school bus driven by Lindell B. Johnson, 24, 3033 Jellison St. No passengers.
>
> VEHICLE NO. 3: Car driven by Ruth L. Anderson, 42, 88 Jefferson Drive. No passengers.
>
> TIME: 9 a.m. today.
>
> LOCATION: Thompson Lane and Lindbergh Avenue.
>
> POLICE RECONSTRUCTION OF EVENT: Bowen was driving west on Thompson Lane. He passed another westbound car that was stopped at a stop sign. Bowen then made a left turn onto Lindbergh Avenue into the path of the school bus. Bus was headed north on Lindbergh. The left side of Bowen's car was struck by the front of the school bus. After the collision, the bus and Bowen's car crossed into the southbound lane and traveled 54 feet north of the intersection, where Bowen's car hit the front end of Anderson's car, which was moving southbound on Lindbergh. That car was forced off the road and into a ditch.
>
> DAMAGE ESTIMATE: Vehicle No. 1 destroyed. Vehicle No. 2 damage estimated at $1,000. Vehicle No. 3 damage estimated at $250. All estimates by police.
>
> DEAD: Kelvin L. Bowen. Died at Springfield Hospital at 7 p.m.
>
> INJURED: Brad Levitt and Ruth L. Anderson, both in satisfactory condition at same hospital.

23. Your instructor will provide you with an accident report or will instruct you to visit your local police department to get one. Write a story from the report. Then prepare a narrative explaining what you would do to prepare a better story if it were to appear in print. Be sure to include information about whom you would contact for more detail and what questions you would ask.

24. Write a fire story from the following information obtained from a fire report:

> BUILDING BURNED: T&L Electronics Co., 4404 U.S. Highway 90.
>
> PERTINENT TIMES: Fire reported at 9:23 p.m. Wednesday. First units arrived at 9:27 p.m. Second alarm issued at 9:42 p.m. Fire under control at 10:56 p.m.
>
> PERSON REPORTING FIRE: Fernando Lopez, 27, of 209 E. Watson Place, night watchman for the company.
>
> INJURIES: None.
>
> ESTIMATED DAMAGE: $1.2 million to building and contents.
>
> PROBABLE CAUSE OF FIRE: Electrical short in main building power supply, according to Capt. Anne Gonzalez, fire marshal.
>
> ADDITIONAL DETAILS: Fire Lt. Steven Gorman, public information officer, reports that the owner of the business, George Popandreau, is on vacation in Florida. Reached by police by phone, he said the building and contents are fully insured. He will return to town tomorrow to begin making arrangements for moving the business to another location and restocking the lost inventory. The fire department used eight vehicles and 45 men in battling the fire. Low water pressure in the area hampered firefighters. New water mains are to be installed in this older area of the city next year.
>
> QUOTE FROM LOPEZ: "I was making my routine rounds when I noticed that it was unusually hot in the rear of the building. Then I turned the corner and saw flames leaping out from a room that contains the electrical circuit breakers, the water heaters and that type of stuff. By the time I got to the phone, the whole back part of the building was on fire. I didn't know a fire could spread that fast."

25. Write a fire story from the following information obtained from a fire report:

> BUILDING BURNED: Residence of Albert Stone, 2935 Parkway Drive.
>
> PERTINENT TIMES: Fire reported at 3:11 a.m. Wednesday. First units arrived at 3:18 a.m. Fire under control at 4:23 a.m.
>
> PERSON REPORTING FIRE: Rowena Stone, daughter of homeowner.
>
> INJURIES: Albert Stone treated for smoke inhalation at Baptist Hospital and admitted for observation. Condition: stable.
>
> ESTIMATED DAMAGE: $25,000 to building and $20,000 to contents.
>
> PROBABLE CAUSE OF FIRE: Careless smoking (Source: Capt. Anne Gonzalez, fire marshal).
>
> ADDITIONAL DETAILS: Rowena Stone, daughter of the injured, was returning home from a date with her boyfriend and noticed smoke coming from the house. She entered immediately and found the house full of smoke and fire in the living room area. She and her boyfriend, Tim Stookey, 21, 309 Lake Lane, were able to get to the bedroom and carry out Albert Stone, who had passed out from consuming too much alcohol, the fire marshal believes. They were able to get Stone out of the house and call the fire department and an ambulance at the home of the next-door neighbor, John Perkins, 2933

Parkway Drive. The fire marshal said there were signs that a cigarette had been left burning in the living room. "The cigarette could have fallen from an ash-tray and ignited the nearby curtains," she said. Mrs. Stone is estranged and believed to be living in California. Her first name is Dorothy. The fire marshal said a full investigation is being conducted.

    INSURANCE DETAILS: House insured by Dominic Prado, agent for Property and Casualty Co., Inc., 303 First Ave. Building insured for $79,000 and contents for $30,000. House valued at $75,000.

26. List all the sources the reporter used to prepare the following story. List other sources that you might have used had you been covering the story. Finally, critique the story, paying particular attention to clarity, concise-ness and writing style.

Horses pull buggies down roads unmarked by tire tracks. Men till fields with horse-drawn plows while the women and children work in the garden. The Amish community near Springfield is a quiet and peaceful island in a hectic and sometimes violent world.

The peace was shattered in May when the Amish community received news of a tragic accident in Fredericksburg, Ohio, that claimed the lives of five Amish children aged 2 to 14 and injured five others. The 10 children were walking home from a birthday party when an 18-year-old driver going 65 mph attempted to pass a truck and barreled into the huddled children.

The Ohio tragedy was a shocking reminder to the Amish here that the refusal to conform to the 21st century can be more than just inconvenient or uncomfortable. On a highway, it can be life-threatening.

Ten members of the Amish in Audrain County, about 20 miles north of Springfield, made the 700-mile trip by van to Ohio.

Valentine Schettler had lived in the Ohio community for 47 years before moving here. He and his son-in-law, Jon Miller, were related to 10-year-old Ruby Troyer, who died in the accident.

About 2,500 Amish from across the nation came to mourn—but not to condemn.

"As Christians, we feel that if we can't forgive, then the Lord can't forgive us," Schettler said. Having to forgive is nothing new for the Amish. Schettler's son lost his wife and daughter in a similar accident in Wisconsin. The families of the children in Ohio have already forgiven the driver, who is charged with five counts of aggravated vehicular homicide. The Amish do not believe in prosecution through the legal system.

"It would not be a very good token of forgiveness," Miller said. Mary Gingerich, who has lived in the local Amish community for 27 years, said the Amish are rarely harassed by local residents. Once, however, she was riding in a buggy when someone in a passing car hurled a soda bottle and hit her in the head. She was holding her year-old baby at the time.

"When things like that happened, we didn't get angry," Gingerich said. "We were just scared."

What really sets the Amish apart is not the refusal to conform to 21st-century technology. It is their ability to forgive those who do them harm, to turn their anger into Christian forbearance.

"I am not angry," Schettler said. "Most of us think it happened for some reason."

27. List all the sources the reporter used to prepare the following story. List other sources that you might have used had you been covering the story. Finally, critique the story, paying particular attention to clarity, concise-ness and writing style.

Lynn Woolkamp knows better than most parents how cars and teenagers can be a tragic combination.

With more than 15 years of experience with the Springfield Police Department and the Lincoln County Sheriff's Department, Woolkamp has seen his share of cracked-up cars and injured teenagers.

The youngest drivers are the ones most often involved in accidents, Woolkamp said. Last year more than 1,100 Lincoln County drivers under 21 were in wrecks, according to the Highway Patrol.

"With the younger drivers, a lot of it is just inexperience," Woolkamp said. "It's kind of a power feeling—you get your license and you've got a little more freedom."

But Woolkamp is doing his best to make sure his own teenage daughter, Kelley, doesn't become part of the statistics.

Since the Rock Haven High School student got her learner's permit in June, her father has given her several hours of behind-the-wheel driving instruction each month. Last week, she turned 16 and picked up her license.

There's some good news and bad news for young drivers like Kelley and their parents.

More young people are in car wrecks, but fewer are dying in the accidents.

Since the state's seat belt law took effect in 1987, traffic deaths of Lincoln County teenagers have decreased by more than half.

From 1988 to 1992, eight Lincoln County residents aged 15 to 19 died in traffic accidents, according to the state Division of Health Resources.

"We have noticed more use of seat belts by our children, and we believe that is why they are walking away," said Don Needham, director of the state's Division of Highway Safety.

Even those who still don't wear seat belts seem to know their own mistake, he explained.

"You'll go to an accident and people will admit to a traffic violation, but not to not having their seat belts on," Needham said. "There'll be a goose egg on their head and a crack in the windshield, and you know they weren't wearing one."

But seat belts don't prevent accidents.

This year, Lincoln County recorded the ninth highest accident rate for young drivers out of the state's 96 counties, according to the Highway Patrol.

The trend is statewide: In 1992, the number of fatal accidents involving young drivers fell by more than 20 percent, despite a 3 percent increase in total auto accidents.

"I think they're starting to depend on the safety devices," Woolkamp said. "Now it's like they think, 'I've got an air bag, so it'll protect me.' With males, there's also a macho thing."

Males account for more than 70 percent of all traffic deaths in the state involving young drivers.

The gender gap is even wider for alcohol-related traffic fatalities.

More than 80 percent of 31 young drivers killed in alcohol-related traffic accidents this past year were male.

"That's staggering considering there are laws that they shouldn't even be purchasing it (alcohol)," Needham said.

Young drivers are involved in alcohol-related deaths at a higher rate than others, according to the National Highway Traffic Safety Administration.

Recently, the state scored a D-plus on a Mothers Against Drunk Driving survey of state efforts to prevent alcohol-related accidents.

But the state Division of Highway Safety disputes the grade. Officials claim the group received inaccurate accident and fatality rates for the state.

But the state doesn't dispute one of MADD's claims: Unlike a growing number of states, this one doesn't have a zero-tolerance law.

In states with such laws, underage drivers with alcohol on their breath can be charged with driving while intoxicated.

"We are hoping to have something introduced in the up-and-coming legislature," Needham said. The proposed measure would classify youths with blood alcohol concentrations of .002 or more as driving while intoxicated.

Woolkamp said it's hard to get young drivers to take safety seriously.

Once he pulled over a young woman for expired plates and wrote her a citation for not wearing a seat belt.

Her father—who had been following behind—pushed back the girl's hair to show scars on her forehead from when she hit the windshield in a previous accident, Woolkamp said.

He said, "You'd think she would've learned."

Obituaries or Life Stories

28. Which elements are missing from the following obituary information? List them in the space provided.

a. John Jones died Saturday night at Springfield Hospital. Funeral services will be at 1:30 p.m. Tuesday. Friends may call at the Black Funeral Home, 2222 E. Broadway Ave., from 6 to 9 p.m. Monday. The Rev. Eugene McCubbins will officiate at services in the Faith Baptist Church. Burial will be at City Cemetery.

b. Mattie Avery, longtime teacher, died at her daughter's home in Springfield. Services will be at 2 p.m. tomorrow at the Springfield Memorial Cemetery.

c. Gary Roets, of Springfield, died Saturday at Springfield Hospital. He was 49. Funeral services will be at 2 p.m. Monday. He is survived by his wife, Jan, and three children: Rebecca, 10; Nathan, 8; and Nicholas, 4. A graduate of the Marquette University School of Law, he practiced law in Springfield for 24 years.

29. Write a lead for an obituary for each of the following people for the *Springfield Daily News* from the information provided below. Assume that the victims are local and will be buried in your city.

a. Jenelle Crookstein, born Jan. 1, 1990, to Don and Jane Crookstein, in Omaha, Neb. The family moved to Springfield in 1988. Jenelle died in a freak skiing accident Sunday while in Vail, Colo. Funeral services will be Wednesday at First Methodist Church at 1 p.m. She was president of her high school student council and of the marching band at the University of Nebraska, where she was a sophomore. She is survived by her parents and a brother, Tom, 10.

b. Pearl Cornell, 73, Rt. 4, Springfield, died yesterday. Was director of Welcome Wagon from 1985 to 1990. Was a volunteer at the Springfield Hospital for 37 years. Was president of the volunteers for seven years. Will be buried today.

c. Jackson Adams died yesterday while watching a high school basketball game in which his son Edward was playing. Apparent heart attack. Jackson was 44. Has two younger sons, 5 and 2. Was a widower. Will be buried tomorrow.

30. Write an obituary for each of the following people from the information given here. At the end of each, indicate what questions, if any, you would need answered.

a. NAME OF FUNERAL HOME: Parker Funeral Service
PHONE: 549-4153
PERSON TO CONTACT: Hal Rice

NAME OF DECEASED: Retired Lt. Col. Ronald H. Lache
ADDRESS: 104 Alhambra Drive, Springfield
OCCUPATION: Retired from the U.S. Air Force
AGE: Born Nov. 3, 1943, at Philadelphia, Pa., to Harry and Thelma
     Curry Lache
CAUSE OF DEATH: Lung cancer
DATE AND PLACE OF DEATH: Monday at his home in Springfield
TIME AND PLACE OF FUNERAL SERVICES: Friday, at Jefferson
     Barracks National Cemetery—Graveside service at 2 p.m.
CONDUCTED BY: Rev. Michael Finney
BURIAL: Jefferson Barracks, Springfield
TIME AND PLACE FOR VISITATION: 7 p.m. Wednesday, Parker
     Funeral Service, 606 Washington Ave.
BIOGRAPHICAL INFORMATION: His wife, the former Delores
     Carney, died March 7 of this year. The family moved to Springfield
     five years ago from Dayton, Ohio. He was a member of the
     Newman Center and the Rock Bridge Lions Club.
SURVIVORS: Survived by his mother, Thelma Lache of Springfield;
     his son, Ronald Lache of Springfield; three daughters—Barbara
     Ann Peck of Dayton, Ohio; Patrice Louis Wylie of Indianapolis, Ind.;
     Cynthia Lache of San Mateo, Calif.

b. NAME OF FUNERAL HOME: Restwell Funeral Service
PHONE: 588-4153
PERSON TO CONTACT: John Kronk

NAME OF DECEASED: Raymond Lee Hope
ADDRESS: 1060 College Ave., Springfield
OCCUPATION: Salesman for Springfield Auto Supply for one year—
     has been in the auto parts business since 1967
AGE: Born July 3, 1925, in Chicago, to Virgil W. and Flossie Dissart
     Hope
CAUSE OF DEATH: Heart attack
DATE AND PLACE OF DEATH: Tuesday, June 17, at Springfield
     Hospital
TIME AND PLACE OF FUNERAL SERVICES: Friday, June 19, at Faith
     Baptist Church at 2 p.m.
CONDUCTED BY: Rev. Eugene McCubbins
BURIAL: Memorial Park Cemetery
TIME AND PLACE FOR VISITATION: 7–9 p.m. Thursday evening at
     Restwell Funeral Service, 307 N. Ninth St.
BIOGRAPHICAL INFORMATION: He and Mary Alice Willett were
     married March 24, 1946, at Chicago, Ill. Lived in Springfield since.
     Served in U.S. Army during World War II.
SURVIVORS: Survived by his wife, Mary, of the home in Springfield;
     his daughter, Mrs. John (Raycene) Bach of Springfield; his brother,
     Earl Hope of Chicago; two granddaughters, Jacqueline and Jennifer
     Bach, both of Springfield

c. Henry Higgins was the victim of a two-car crash Friday night at the
     corner of U.S. 63 and Route NN in rural Lincoln County. The driver of
     the other car, Thomas Henry, 32, is hospitalized with head and neck
     injuries in Springfield Hospital. Although he was young, Higgins had

accomplished much. He was president of his senior class at Springfield High School, he was a letterman for two years for the University of Illinois football team for which he played tight end, and he recently earned his real estate license and was associated with the firm of West and Haver, Springfield. He was a member of the Springfield Jaycees. Survivors include wife, Cloris, 209 Fourth St.; his parents, Ralph and Amy Higgins, of Springfield; a sister, Ruth, of Birmingham, Ala.; and a brother, Russell, of St. Louis.

Funeral services will be held Tuesday at the Newman Center with Father Ralph Green officiating. Burial will be in City Cemetery. Higgins was born Sept. 24, 1985, in Springfield. He lived there all his life. Friends may call at the Restwell Funeral Home from 7 to 10 p.m. Monday.

31. The best-written obituaries often require additional reporting.
    a. An obituary notice from a funeral home contains all the basic information. However, under biographical information, it indicates only that the man worked at the local paper mill for 25 years. If you wanted to find out whether there was anything extraordinary about this man, whom would you call, and why? Where might that call lead you?

    b. An obituary notice contains most of the basic information. The age of the deceased is 14. There is nothing under cause of death. Memorials are requested for the American Cancer Society. What angle does this information suggest may be possible? Whom would you call, and why?

    c. On the funeral home's obituary notice, the space under biographical information is empty. The deceased has no local survivors. Whom would you call, and what would you be looking for?

32. Important policy questions often arise when you are writing obituaries.
    a. If a private citizen commits suicide on the grounds of a local high school one night when no one is around, would you include the cause of death in the obituary? Why or why not?

b. If the mayor dies and you can quote other city officials as saying the mayor's drinking had interfered with his work in the last year, would you include that in the obituary? Why or why not?

c. If a citizen who was an active member of several civic groups dies and you have several paragraphs describing the work she did for the community, would you include the fact that she had died of AIDS? Why or why not?

33. CHALLENGE EXERCISE
Search your library for information on the 1954 murder trial of Dr. Sam Sheppard in Cleveland, Ohio. Then find a story in your local newspaper library about a local case in which there was a change of venue (where the trial was moved to another city). How do the issues in the local case compare with those in the Sheppard case?

34. CHALLENGE EXERCISE
Using computer-based online services to search for information, write a 1,000-word report on the highway accident rate in your state. Contrast that with the accident rates in other similar states.

35. CHALLENGE EXERCISE
Using information from a database search, write a two-page advance obituary for one of the following. At the end, list your sources.
a. Anderson Cooper
b. Phil Collins
c. Derek Jeter
d. Louis Farrakhan
e. Javier Arenas
f. Margaret Thatcher
g. Your mayor
h. Your college or university president
i. Your instructor
j. Maya Lin

Law

14

1. Nonjournalists sometimes ask why our profession deserves special protection in the U.S Constitution. How would you answer that question?

2. The First Amendment protects five freedoms. What are they, and how are they related to one another?

3. **a.** Define "libel."

   b. What four categories do courts use to determine if a person's reputation has been damaged?

   c. What are three traditional defenses for the press in a libel action?

d. What kind of protection from libel suits do the courts allow members of the three branches of government?

4. In the "On the Job" feature in Chapter 14 of the text, lawyer and journalist Ken Paulson suggests that reporters ask themselves four questions as a safeguard against libel. What protection can those four questions provide?

5. a. What are the differences between the *Butts* case and the *Walker* case?

b. Define "public official."

c. Define "public figure."

6. The Internet raises new legal issues for journalists, including bloggers. Identify a major issue, and discuss its significance.

7. Visit the WikiLeaks site (wikileaks.org), and read some news reports about the organization and its history. What opportunities does the organization create for journalism, and what are the legal and ethical problems it poses?

8. On three occasions, you observe the mayor of your community in a local nightclub, where it appears he has been drinking too much. Two council members tell you they believe the mayor is an alcoholic, but they won't let you use their names. What additional information, if any, would you try to gather before deciding whether to print the story?

9. Many journalists support the passage of shield laws, which give protection against the revealing of confidential sources. What arguments might a journalist make against a state or federal shield law?

10. Determine whether any passages in the following story are libelous. If you believe you have found a libelous passage, describe what you would need to do to print it or whether you would omit it.

> A sophomore at Springfield University claims a chemistry professor has sexually harassed her.
>
> Cindy Watring, 123 Columbus Hall, says the professor, David Moore, has touched her during tutoring sessions in his office and has invited her to his apartment several times. She said she declined his invitations.
>
> "I am having trouble in the class, and I have to go see him to get help with my papers and projects," she said. "But I am scared to go in his office now."
>
> Moore denied having any improper contact with the student and threatened this newspaper with a libel suit if it published the story.
>
> Watring said she is thinking of filing a formal complaint with the university. "I don't know how to do that," she said. "I just don't know what to do."

11. Determine whether any of the passages in the following story are potentially libelous. If any are, explain what you would do to print the information or whether you would leave it out.

Provost Ronald Kemper has been asked to resign, sources have told the *Campus Voice*.

Kemper declined to talk to the *Voice* about the situation, but sources close to him say that he will announce his resignation in two days.

An administrative source told the *Voice* that Chancellor Bernadette Anderson has asked Kemper to resign because of widespread faculty dissatisfaction with the job he has been doing.

"He has lost the confidence of the faculty," the administrator said. "He can't get any administrative proposals through the faculty because they don't trust him."

Through a spokesperson, Chancellor Anderson denied that she has asked for Kemper's resignation.

A member of the Faculty Senate, Mary Barnridge, an assistant professor of English, said several faculty members think Kemper should leave. "He tried to cram a proposal to eliminate several programs down our throats. He didn't want our reaction; he just wanted approval," she said. "The faculty got turned off by the way he handled the situation."

Two other faculty members who declined to be identified agreed with Barnridge.

"He's a lost cause," a professor of Spanish said. "We just don't believe anything he says."

Kemper became provost 11 years ago.

12. Are any passages in the following story potentially libelous? If so, identify them and cite evidence to support your evaluation.

The Planning and Zoning Commission haggled over the proposed energy ordinance Wednesday and decided it was unresearched, unenforceable and unfair.

In a 6–2 vote, the commission recommended that the City Council defeat the bill when the council votes on it next month. Marjorie Cox and Chester Edwards cast the dissenting votes.

Larry Niedergerke, acting chairman, instructed Edwards and Cox to draw up a dissenting resolution for the council to balance the commission's recommendation.

The proposed ordinance would require weather-stripping, new insulation for water heaters and air ducts, and new minimal levels for roofs. The council sent the ordinance to six advisory panels earlier this year for recommendations.

So far only the Community Development Commission has approved the ordinance.

P&Z Commissioner Keith Schrader said the proposed ordinance does not demonstrate cost-effectiveness, and he questioned whether its requirements would be a sound investment for homeowners.

"I would really like to know how much money would be spent on insulation as opposed to how much saved," Schrader said.

Schrader said he is not completely opposed to an energy ordinance, but he needs to see hard figures before he supports the ordinance.

Edwards agreed that the ordinance should be researched more carefully but said that some sort of ordinance is necessary.

"I think we all need to be good stewards of our natural resources," he said. "There are some things in this ordinance that I don't like, but I just didn't want to vote it down."

Cox said higher standards are necessary to make homeowners and landlords save on energy costs.

Nonetheless, enforcement is what caused many commissioners to voice their opposition to the proposal.

"I'm very much in favor of letting people make their own decisions, and their own mistakes at times, rather than (resorting to) legislation," Rex Campbell said.

Clayton Johnson agreed. "We can't tell people to put on an extra sweater or long underwear, but we might as well if we are going to legislate one of these items," he said.

"It just seems to me that we are waiting for God and government to take care of us, and I don't think that should be."

"Bill Rodgers wrote this thing, and it's pretty clear to me that Bill Rodgers is a fool," said Commissioner Robert Cummings.

Rodgers is a city staff member who works in the Planning Department.

13. What passages in the following story are potentially libelous, and why?

KENNETT SQUARE, Pa. (UPI)—The doctor heading the team investigating the death of Kentucky Derby winner Swale said Wednesday the cause of death may never be known. However, Dr. Helen Acland would not rule out the possibility of foul play.

Acland, chief of the Laboratory of Large Animal Pathology at the University of Pennsylvania's New Bolton Center, said tests on tissues taken from the three-year-old colt did not reveal the cause of death.

She said examination of the tissues, taken during an autopsy performed hours after Swale collapsed and died Sunday at Belmont Park near New York, supported preliminary findings that ruled out a heart attack as the cause of death.

"We found an enlargement of the heart that is usually found in athletes," Acland said during a news conference at the rural facility, 40 miles outside of Philadelphia. "We also found microscopic lesions of the liver and kidneys but not severe enough to contribute to the demise of the animal.

"It's possible we may never know the cause of death. There are some things that can cause death in horses that don't leave a trace."

Acland said her "gut feeling" was that the horse died of a "cardiac dysfunction, but we may never be able to confirm that. There are other things that can make the heart stop besides a heart attack."

Acland did not rule out foul play in the death of Swale. She said extensive toxicological tests would have to be done to determine if poisoning was involved, and those tests still could prove inconclusive.

"I'd be able to answer that better in a few weeks after we've gone through a range of chemical tests," she said. "Judging the history of the animal, he seemed to be well taken care of. The possibility (of foul play) is small, but I have trouble defining small. I'd like to defer that question until we've performed some testing."

14. Write a story based on the following information. Be sure to eliminate anything that is potentially libelous.

Mark Dillow, 43, of 209 Perch Lane, has been charged with violating the city's rental-housing license ordinance. The offense carries a possible sentence of a fine of up to $1,000 and six months in jail. The ordinance calls for inspection and subsequent licensing of rental housing to ensure that minimal standards are met.

City inspectors, acting on a complaint from tenant John Bowers, 21, of 303A Court Drive, found that the apartment was not licensed and had not been previously inspected. An inspection revealed 17 fire and safety hazards in Bowers' apartment alone. The city has informed Dillow it will inspect three remaining apartments at 303 Court Drive next week.

City Prosecutor Mel Cross said the case will be heard in Municipal Court Monday. Dillow would not comment, but he will be defended by Joan Anderson, a local attorney who handles all of Dillow's legal work.

This is the first time the city has taken a landlord to court since the inspection law went into effect in January.

City Housing Inspector Richard Laventhol said, "I've never seen so many violations in one spot. There were frayed electrical wires, leaky toilets, you name it. The place was disgusting. A guy who allows his property to get run down like that should be sent up the river. It's not fair to the tenants."

The city prosecutor would give no further comment.

15. Browsing through the website of a newspaper from another campus, you see an article that you would like to publish on your campus newspaper's website. You don't see any copyright notice on the newspaper. Do you need permission? Do you need permission if you credit the source? Why or why not? Is linking to the source a good option? Why or why not?

16. You are the editor of a newspaper in a town of 65,000 people. One of your reporters has just given you a story about the public administrator, the elected official who is appointed by courts to administer the affairs of people who die without wills or people judged mentally incompetent to manage their own affairs. The administrator manages thousands of dollars' worth of assets from the estates of the deceased and similar amounts in holdings of the mentally incompetent. Your reporter has learned that once the administrator was elected, she transferred all of these accounts to one of the five local banks. Further, the bank in question lists the public administrator as a minor stockholder (less than 1 percent). The state's conflict-of-interest law is weak and does not clearly extend to public administrators. Discuss the legal implications of publishing the story. Then discuss the issues of fairness. Even if there is no problem with libel if you publish the story, is it fair to the administrator to do so? Consider that earnings on the accounts in question would not be nearly enough to cause an increase in the earnings of a minority stockholder of the bank.

17. **CHALLENGE EXERCISE**
    Which U.S. Supreme Court decision has been most important to freedom of the press? Write a two-page report explaining the case you choose and justifying your choice.

15 Ethics

1. Three broad philosophical approaches can provide answers to ethical questions: the ethics of duty, the ethics of final ends and situation ethics. Use these three approaches to work through the following situations.

   a. A terrorist snatches a youth in a ticket line at the local airport and demands to be given passage to a foreign country. You have been sent to the airport to cover the live event. The terrorist has warned the police and the press to stay back, but you are confident that you could get film of the terrorist without his knowing it. Describe how the three philosophies would guide you in making your decision.

   b. You are a photographer for a newspaper in a city of 200,000. An explosion occurs at a factory employing dozens of local residents. Many of the employees' family members, obviously distraught, are waiting at the police department for word on their relatives. Most are crying; some are nearly hysterical. Do you approach any of these people and ask to photograph them? Or do you photograph them without speaking to them? Explain your answer, and identify the philosophical approach that best describes your response.

c. You learn as a reporter that one or more people have been painting swastikas on houses in a mostly Jewish neighborhood. You interview people in the neighborhood, and they beg you not to take photos or write a story for fear that media coverage will only encourage others to commit hate crimes in the neighborhood. Would you withhold the information or any part of it? Identify the philosophical approach that best describes your response.

2. Use the Potter Box to reach a decision about the following ethical situations. In step three of the box, show how at least four ethical principles apply. Do not use the same principles for each of the cases.

a. SITUATION
Four sources, all of whom demand anonymity, tell you that a married candidate for governor in your state is having an affair with one of her campaign workers. You have no information from anyone other than these anonymous sources, all of whom are quite reliable and unconnected with the gubernatorial race. Should you run the story? Should you include the names of the informants?

VALUES

PRINCIPLES
(1)

(2)

(3)

(4)

LOYALTIES

JUDGMENT

b. SITUATION

A colleague on your news staff has written a blog that was published online. As you read it, you discover that a couple of sentences seem familiar. You do some investigating and find that your colleague has plagiarized from a newspaper column. What do you do?

VALUES

PRINCIPLES

(1)

(2)

(3)

(4)

LOYALTIES

JUDGMENT

c. SITUATION
   You are a reporter for a television station. A man calls to tell you that
   he is going to set himself on fire because his wife and children left him
   and he has lost everything. He tells you the time and place where he
   is going to do this. Would you tell him you would not come? Call the
   police? Try to talk him out of it? Go there with an experienced coun-
   selor? Ask him not to call anyone else?

VALUES

PRINCIPLES
(1)

(2)

(3)

(4)

LOYALTIES

d. SITUATION
You are a television camera operator. You are the first journalist to arrive at a river where two officers are trying to save a child from drowning. You can swim, and they could use your help. Would you shoot the scene, or would you set down the camera and help save the child?

VALUES

PRINCIPLES
(1)

(2)

(3)

(4)

LOYALTIES

JUDGMENT

e. SITUATION
An elderly woman calls the city desk and asks the newspaper not to publish her name or address in the story about a burglary at her home. She is afraid because she lives alone. Would you carry out your paper's policy of carrying her full name, age and address? Use only her name but no address? Comply with her request?

VALUES

PRINCIPLES
(1)

(2)

(3)

(4)

LOYALTIES

JUDGMENT

f. SITUATION
Car repair shops in a college town are suspected of telling students that their cars need unnecessary repairs that often cost hundreds of dollars. Your editor asks you to loosen a spark plug wire on your car and take it to five garages to find out what they would charge to fix the engine's problem. At the very first garage you visit, the mechanic asks, "You're not a reporter, are you?" What would you say?

VALUES

PRINCIPLES
(1)

(2)

(3)

(4)

LOYALTIES

JUDGMENT

g. SITUATION

A photographer who works for you has been "caught" using Photoshop to alter images. What would you tell him or her about this practice?

VALUES

PRINCIPLES

(1)

(2)

(3)

(4)

JUDGMENT

3. While writing a feature story, you find some excellent quotes about your subject from another written source. May you use those quotes as if you obtained them yourself, or must you credit the other written source? What if you found the quotes on a website?

4. Do you think the code of ethics for public relations professionals should be different from the code of ethics for journalists? Why or why not?

5. You are a news anchor for a television station that inserts video news releases, known as VNRs, into its news broadcast without telling viewers that these are VNRs. Would you protest this practice, or do you regard it as acceptable?

6. Do you think the news organization for which you will work should have a code of ethics? Why or why not? How should a news organization enforce its code of ethics?

7. CHALLENGE EXERCISE
Do an Internet search for codes of ethics for journalists. After studying them, compose the major points of your own code of ethics.

APPENDIX 1
Exercises for Copy Editing and Proofreading Symbols

1. Edit the following story using the correct copy editing symbols.

Cole County officials will exhume the body of an eldelry man to determine whether there is any connection between his death and a Springfield man arrested here on charges of first-degree robbery and of kidnapping an 85-year-old Lincoln County woman.

Authorities said Sprngfield resident Eric Barnhouse, 28, an insurance salesman, may be connected to the death death of the Cole County man, the disappearance of a Troy woman, the assault of a Warrenton woman and the death of a Fulton woman. He also was charged with stealing money from an elderly Boonville woman.

Barnhouse contacted the Cole County man just before the man's death, said Richard Lee, an investigator with the Cole County prosecuting attorney's office. Cole County officials are looking for anything that may lead to a suspicious cause of death, Lee said.

"There was no autopsy performed at the time of death, so we're not sure what the cause of death was," Lee said.

No charges have been filed in the Cole County case.

Earlier this week Springfield police played host to a meeting of area law enforcement officials interested in sharing information about Barnhouse. Since then, more charges have been filed, and Barnhouse is suspected of being involved in several other cases.

Barnhouse was already being held in the Lincoln County Jail when Springfield police served him a Warren County warrant Jan. 9 for 1stdegree burglary. Officers also charged him with resisting arrest and with probation violation from a previous Lincoln county burglary conviction.

Police served Barnhouse with another warrant Wednesday charging him with kidnapping and burglary of a Lincoln County woman. Barnhouse was invited into the local woman's home on December 31 after he identified him-self as an insurance agent, police said.

According to police, Barnhouse returned to the woman's home later that day and asked her for a check for 3 insurance premiums. The woman refused, and he held her at gunpoint and demanded she go to the bank and cash a check.

After driving around Springfield for several hours with the victim, the woman gave Barnhouse $60, and he returned her to her home un-harmed.

When Springfield police arrested Barnhouse on Jan. 9, they discovered the purse of a woman who disappeared the same day from her home in Troy, which is 50 miles northwest of St. Louis.

Springfield police also believe Barnhouse posed as an insurance agent Jan. 7 to an 84-year-old woman in Warrenton.

According to the victim's statement, she was beaten unconscious. He had placed a rag with some type of liquid over her mouth before she passed out, she said.

Fulton police are waiting for a toxicologist's report on the death of an elderly woman they believe Barnhouse called on before she died. Barnhouse attempted to cash a check from the woman's account, said Mick Herbert, Fulton police chief. Results of her autopsy were inconclusive.

2. Edit the following story using the correct copy editing symbols.

        Springfield police have arrested a local woman three times in the last 9 months, most recently on Thursday in connection with the December attempted robbery of a taxi driver.

        Willa Walter, 34, of 3601 W. Ash Street was arrested by Springfield police at 2:52 a.m. Thursday. Police "had not even considered her as a suspect" before receiving a Crimestoppers E-mail tip Wednesday, Capt. Dennis Veach said. Walter remained in the Lincoln County Jail on Thursday afternoon in lieu of $25,000 bail.

        Police arrested Walter for the Dec. 14 attempted robbery of a Bob's Checker Cab. The taxi driver had delivered a woman to the intersection of Garth Ave. and Sexton Rd., Veach said, when she pulled out a revolver and demanded money. After a brief struggle, the woman fled without the cash. At the time of the incident, Walter was free on bond from another armed robbery arrest, this one involving the April 9 holdup of a Texaco gas station at 2102 W. Ash St. Springfield police arrested her a few hours after the robbery, thanks to a witness at the gas station who wrote down her car's license plate number. She pleaded guilty Nov. 30.

        But Walter and the police met again fairly soon. Less than a month later, Walter was arrested again, this time on misdemeanor theft, assault and marijuana possession charges. She awaits sentencing for those charges Feb. 25.

3. Correct the following story using the proper proofreading symbols.

        A Crime Stopper call helped police find a suspect in the Tuesday shooting of a 28-year-old Springfield man.

        Police arrested Aaron Brewster, 24, of St. Balentine on Firday at about 10 a.m.

Police received a call about a shooting on Allen Walkway about 9:55 P.m. Tuesday. They arrived and found a man on the ground with a single gunshot wound just above the heart, said Cpt. Chris Egbert of the Springfield Police Department.

Following surgery, the victim was in stable condition at Linocon County Hospital on Friday. Police did not know his condition Saturrday.

Brewster had been staying in Springfield for a few months but calls St. Balentine his home, said Sgt. Bill Haws.

The shooting, which occurred near the victims house, was the result of an argument about a female friend of the two men. Several people were present, including the woman over whom they were arguing, Haws said.

Police arrested Brewster without incident at 908 North Garth Ave.

Brewster remained in the Lincoln County Jail on Saturday on charges of probation and parole violation, armed criminal action and firstdegree assault. Bond has not been set.

4. Correct the following story using the proper proofreading symbols.

Springfield police arrested a local woman on suspicion of forging and cashing bogus payrroll checks at area supermarkets.

Shirley M. Hannah of 1301 Ridge Road was released from Lincoln County Jail after posting a $45,000 bond, a sheriff's department spokesman said.

Hannah, 21 was arrested Saturday after an employee of Food Barn, 705 Business Loop 70 West, recognized her because she'd previously bounced a check at the store, Sgt. Dean France said.

France said investigators believe Hannah was working with at least one other person for about a week. Capt. Mick Covington said they opened a fake business account at a Springfield bank to obtain bogus payroll checks

"It appears someone opened a fraudulent account in the same name as a legitimate company, France said. He said Hannah is suspected of cashing at least twelve checks.

APPENDIX 2
Exercises for
Wire Service Style

1. Correct the following sentences for capitalization where necessary.

   a. Barack Obama chose Hillary Clinton as his Secretary of State.

   b. His Jeep was the last one the Army had.

   c. The California and Oregon Legislatures blamed each other for the stream's condition.

   d. In the Vietnam war, the U.S. feared intervention by the Chinese.

   e. The all-stars included Outfielder Alfonso Soriano of the Chicago Cubs.

   f. The justice department said it would not appeal the decision.

   g. The Rocky mountains are the dominant geological feature of the West.

   h. The latin population is the fastest-growing in the region.

   i. She prefers Roquefort cheese on her crackers.

   j. The fm band is now the most popular on radio.

2. Correct the following sentences for capitalization where necessary.

   a. She bought a jeep so she would have no trouble in the desert.

   b. Ramon sought a realtor for help in locating a house.

   c. The store was at Kon Tiki and Ridgelea streets.

   d. The tv was tuned in to the Royals-Yankees game.

   e. Martinez said, "it will be a while before you see that again."

   f. "Give me a kleenex," said the teenager.

   g. Jeremiah Wright, former pastor of Barack Obama, was a controversial figure during the 2008 election.

h. "I'd walk a mile for a camel," the cigarette commercial actor said.

i. Christians believe that Jesus Christ is the son of god.

j. For Muslims, Allah is the name of the deity.

3. Correct the following sentences for capitalization where necessary.

    a. She placed the bowl of jello in the frigidaire.

    b. The army jeep collided with a car at Fifth and Elm streets.

    c. "Let's have a coke," the realtor said.

    d. The Tennessee and Mississippi Legislatures voted for repeal.

    e. The Montana Legislature will convene today.

    f. "It was a tough decision," the President said.

    g. Donald Rumsfeld was the Secretary of Defense during part of George W. Bush's Administration.

    h. "They were the best passing team we've seen all year," said cornerback Eric Wright.

    i. He was described as a Greek God.

    j. God is merciful because he forgives.

4. Following the guidelines for abbreviation, correct these sentences where necessary.

    a. Memphis, Tenn., and Kansas City, Kan., are a day's drive apart.

    b. He lives at 1042 South Demaret Drive in Milwaukee, Wisc.

    c. Ortega moved to 322 Orange St. SE in Pittsburgh, Penn.

    d. Ms. Santana is a rich woman, according to *Business Week*.

    e. USC is in Los Angeles, Cal.

    f. The C.I.A. is supposed to avoid domestic activities, which the FBI handles.

    g. He was going 65 m.p.h. in a 30 mph zone.

    h. Antigua, WI, is a cold place in the winter, she said.

i. Let's watch TV when we get to Cheyenne, WY, tonight.

j. The U.S. ambassador to the United Nations told him to forget it.

5. Following the guidelines for abbreviation, correct these sentences where necessary.

a. All who attended were from Honolulu, Hawaii, and Dallas, Tex.

b. Jackson, Ms., was the scene of the confrontation.

c. He is a native of Lawrence, Kans.

d. The deadline is March 19, but may be extended to Apr. 1.

e. John lives at 302 South Trenton Blvd.

f. He was driving at 90 m.p.h.

g. It was the worst winter storm since January 12, 1977.

h. Mr. and Mrs. Aurelio Rodriguez were the guests of Ms. Maude Clinton.

i. He was to appear on K.S.D.-T.V.

j. The fire destroyed the home at 396 Bluff Drive S.W.

6. Correct all improper punctuation in the following sentences.

a. "Tell him I said 'Forget it,' when you see him," Jones said.

b. Grapes of Wrath is one of the most popular books of all time.

c. "TV Guide" is the best-selling magazine in the United States.

d. "Tell him there are no more grapes", Dreiling said.

e. It is the best thing to do, and I think it will work.

f. She said it couldn't be done but we did it.

g. Survivors include his wife, Helen; three sons, John, Devin and Richard, and two grandsons.

h. He spent three more years in prison after serving a 10 year term for burglary.

i. The best movies were made in the 1960's, he said.

7. Correct all improper punctuation in the following sentences.

   a. James Michener wrote the novel "Hawaii".

   b. All the boys attended (except John.).

   c. Dr. Ralph Simpson, Jr. started practice in May 1978.

   d. President Kennedy was killed Nov. 22, 1963 in Dallas.

   e. She has lived in Omaha, Neb., and Kansas City, Mo.

   f. The 8 and 9 year old girls will practice baseball today.

   g. He threw a 90 yard touchdown pass for a last second victory.

   h. The heavily-damaged car was towed away.

   i. "Where is the grocery store?," he asked.

   j. It was the worst three-year period since the 1920's.

8. Correct the use of numerals in the following sentences.

   a. He is the Number One quarterback in Tennessee this year.

   b. Oregonians cast 34,546 votes for Rodgers and only 3156 for Contrell.

   c. There were six people in the party of fourteen who had been there before.

   d. There is a chain of convenience stores known as 7-Eleven, and the name is spelled that way.

   e. The temperature was 89 degrees in the shade.

   f. I'd walk a thousand miles for a drink of water right now.

   g. The survey results changed only .04 percent from one month to the next.

   h. The prime minister lives at No. 10 Downing Street.

   i. There are only three sergeants left in the platoon.

   j. 1492 was the year Columbus arrived with 3 ships.

9. Correct the use of numerals in the following sentences.

   a. The Yankees won the game 10 to three.

   b. He is the No. 1 astronaut in the space shuttle program.

   c. The temperature dropped 6 degrees in four hours for an overnight low

      of 27.

   d. There were four Missourians, three Kansans and 14 Oklahomans at the

      meeting.

   e. John Dillon, 26, of 206 Willow Way, won three percent of the vote.

   f. He had five dollars in his pocket and $6 in his hand.

   g. U.S. Highway One parallels the East Coast.

   h. He said he would be there at six p.m., but he did not arrive until 8.

   i. The unemployment rate dropped .7 percent to 6.2 percent.

   j. He lives on 10th Street near the 5th Avenue intersection.

10. Correct the errors in spelling, punctuation, capitalization and other areas
    of style in the following sentences.

    a. The New York and New Jersey Legislators could not agree on a solution.

    b. Eau Claire, Wis. and Rapid City, S.Dak. both are college towns.

    c. The San Diego Padres and the Los Angeles Dodgers are tied for the lead

       in the West and the St. Louis Cardinals lead the Central.

    d. Roger Federer and Venus Williams dominated the world of tennis this

       year.

    e. Brigadier General Paul Ramos and Financier Hougala Mugaba met

       secretly in the Caribbean.

    f. San Francisco was well-equipped to treat victims of Aids because of its

       large gay community and the expertise of doctors there.

    g. Wilmington, Delaware, is the home of many corporations because of

       Delaware's lenient incorporation laws.

h. The Miami Herald is one of the nation's best at covering the situation in Latin America; the Herald's large hispanic readership is interested in news of that area.

i. A tornado tore through Jonesboro, Ark., today and caused damage estimated in the millions of dollars.

j. South Africa's policy of apartheid was repugnant to most Americans.

k. The Abilene (Tex.) Reporter-News was aggressive in covering the activities of financier T. Boone Pickens.

l. The New Mexico Lobos scored a last-minute touchdown Saturday to upset the Arizona Wildcats 24 to 21.

m. "Grapes of Wrath" was one of John Steinbeck's great novels.

n. Athens, Ga., is the home of the Number One Georgia Bulldogs.

o. "Hockey Night in Canada" is one of the top rated shows in that **country**.

p. The Denver Broncos captured the imagination of the Mountain States with their last-minute heroics.

q. America's Cup is the most highly coveted trophy in yachting.

r. The Beatles were a hit in their hometown of Liverpool, England, before vaulting to stardom in the United States and elsewhere around the World.

s. Juventus, a team in the Italian soccer league, won that country's championship.

t. The North Carolina Tarheels are consistently one of the best teams in college basketball.

u. Halley's Comet captured the country's imagination with its appearance in 1986.

v. Kansas State University in Manhattan, Kan., has been a Big XII power in basketball for many years.

w. Killer whales are misnamed; they really are mild-mannered creatures.

x. Willard Scott of NBC's Today show probably is the nation's best-known weatherman.

y. When its time to sell the house, I'm going to call a realtor.

11. Correct the spelling and style errors in the following sentences using the appropriate copy editing symbols.

a. The best place to eat in Rattatan, Wisc. was a place called The Brat, he said, but it went out of business last year.

b. Fort Hays, Kansas was a calvary outpost in the 1800's.

c. Brewing companies spend millions of dollars on TV advertising each year, according to advertising industry experts.

d. Sergeants earn more than corporals in the US army, and they earn more than lieutenatns in the Russian army.

e. Ricardo gutierrez rode the quarterhourse to victory in the local county fair race.

f. 1984 was an election year, she told the delegates, so no texes were raised.

g. He became a first class scout in the first year he was eligible.

h. More than 4,900,000 people live in that state, according to the latest figures from the United States Bureau of the census.

i. The first full year of the war 1942 was a devastating one for American morale.

j. John Wayne was an American institution for years, but he won an oscar only in the last year of his life.

k. "When you go out, be sure to take the garbage", he said.

l. Its ridiculous that no boy from that school has ever been a starting quarterback at a major collefge considering the success of the program.

m. The outfieldder hit .268 in his last full seson in the magors before the leg injury halted his careeer.

12. Correct the style errors in the following stories using the appropriate copy editing symbols.

A. WASHINGTON (AP)—The Treasury Department is considering restricting each American to three Federally-insured banks, savings institutions or credit unions—no matter how little money is in each.

The department asked the Federal Deposit Insurance Corp. to estimate how much the proposal would save and to describe potential problems in administering it, the F.D.I.C.'s Chairman, L. William Seidman, said today.

The Independent Bankers Assn. of America is vigorously fighting it.

B. WASHINGTON (AP)—Home building plunged by six percent in October, the Commerce Department said today, extending the longest construction slide on record and sinking housing starts to their lowest level since the 1981-82 recession.

Industry analysts cited shrinking consumer confidence and the growing inability of builders to get credit as causes of the 9-month drop, the longest since the Government began keeping track in 1959. Many analysts expect the slide to continue into mid-1991, especially in light of a broader weakening of the economy.

13. Correct the style errors in the following story using the appropriate copy editing symbols.

At least one person is dead and six injured after a two-car wreck Wednesday evening on U.S. Highway 40 west of Midway that brought out state troopers, four paramedic units and 35 Lincoln County firefighters.

Three injured were transported to Springfield Hospital, where one was listed in critical condition late Wednesday, and 2 were listed in serious condition.

Three others were taken to Lincoln Hospital Center. Hospital officials refused to discuss their conditions.

One of the injured also suffered a heart attack, said Rob Brown, a Lincoln County Fire Protection District spokesperson. That person was in cardiac arrest at the scene, with no pulse or vital signs, Brown said.

Brown described the seven victim's injuries as ranging from mild back and neck problems to internal injuries. "I'm sure there were broken bones," he said.

A red Chevrolet Nova ran a stop sign at the corner of Ballard Road and Highway 40 and hit a red Ford Escort, which was moving west on Highway 40, said state trooper Charles Schaffer. Police said the intersection has a history of bad accidents.

Both cars landed in a wide ditch on the north side of the highway. The Escort landed on its roof. Some of the passengers in both cars were thrown from the vehicles.

Police would not identify the drivers or the injured, pending notification of relatives. Witnesses said those involved in the wreck were as young as 10 years of age.

Danny Allenbaugh and Marco Arrendondo, two Fayette High School students, were among the first to arrive at the scene following the accident.

They parked their vehicle so its headlights would face both wrecked cars. The lights shone on one of the victims, a girl, who was lying in front of their car.

While they waited for ambulances to arrive, the students helped two women who were trapped in the upended Escort get out of the car.

The women, both students at Central Methodist College, did not seem to be seriously injured, Allenbaugh said.

14. Correct the style errors in the following story using the appropriate copy editing symbols.

Gusty winds fanned the flames of a fire Thursday afternoon that caused $30,000 dollars' damage to a boardinghouse on Paris Road.

Firefighters rescued one resident from the second floor by ladder and another from the basement, said Lieutenant James Daugherty of the Springfield Fire Dept.

No one in the house at 1308 Paris Road was injured, Daugherty said, but a fireman broke a toe while working on the ladder.

At one point, all the city's major fire-fighting vehicles were present for the three-alarm fire, said a firefighter on the scene.

The first alarm came in at 3:32 p.m. The blaze was brought under control in fifty minutes.

Daugherty said damage to the house was mostly on the second and third floors. Careless smoking on a couch was listed as the probable cause of the fire by fire department officials.

"We've got our work cut out for us now," said R. J. Newell, owner of the house, as he stood out front surveying the damaged green and yellow building. "A lot of money there, that's what this looks like to me."

He had just finished repairing an ice machine when one of his tenants found him at work and told him the house was burning, he said. "They told me that was more important than what I was doing."

Newell, who runs a general maintenance company in Springfield, said the tenants would help him repair the damage. "They don't have anyplace else to go," he said. "That's why they're here."

"Everybody will probably pitch in," Newell said. "Cooking, cleaning, building, something."

The three-story building contains 11 apartments, Newell said. 16 people were living there at the time of the fire, he said.

Several residents of the house stood across the street and watched the firefighters working. Most were worried about their possessions.

"I've got a guitar down there," said John Kendrick, who has lived in the basement for eight months.

15. Correct the style errors in the following story using the appropriate copy editing symbols.

A 39-year-old Springfield man was robbed early Thursday at gunpoint while making a deposit at Century State Bank, 2114 Paris Rd., according to police reports.

The victim, an employee of Pizza Hut, was making a night deposit at about 1:30 A.M. when a pickup truck with two men drove into the bank parking lot.

The passenger in the pickup was wearing a mask made of a see-thru fabric similar to panty hose, said Capt. Dennis Veach of the Springfield Police Dept. The passenger got out of the truck, pulled out a hand-gun and then demanded the victim's money.

The victim handed over the cash, and the suspects drove away on Whitegate Dr.

The robbers are both white males. The driver was heavy-set and had short, dark blonde hair. The passenger was wearing blue jeans and an unknown color jacket.

Veach said Thursday's robbery doesn't appear to be linked to two other robberies of pizza store employees in the past week. A Domino's Pizza delivery person was robbed Tuesday night at gunpoint at Ashwood Apts., 1201 Ashland Road. The victim, a 19-year-old woman, was walking back to her car at 9:30 p.m. after delivering a pizza when she was robbed.

On Dec. 27, a Domino's Pizza employee was robbed by a man with a single-barreled shotgun. That robber entered the Domino's at 3102 Green Meadows Way just before midnight.

CrimeStoppers is seeking information leading to the arrest of the suspects in the robberies. They are offering a reward and guarantee anonymity. CrimeStoppers is at 555-8477.

16. Correct the various types of errors in the following story using the appropriate copy editing symbols.

The spell of hot, dry weather that has hedl the area in it's grasp for the last few few weeks is taking its tole on grasslands and fire fighters.

Saturday, in the wake of 15- and 25-mph winds and a high temperature of 99 degrees, fire protection agencies from across the area responded to sixteen calls.

At the largest of those, a 25-acre grass fire on Peabody Road north of Prathersville and west of Route 19, paramedics treated on sight at least five of 35 fire fighters for heat exhaustion, county fire chief Debra Schuster said.

Three mroe of the heavily-clad firefighters were hospitalized for heat exhaustion, and two of those were flown to Springfield Hospital by helicopter. All were treated for about 1 hour and released.

Dennis Sapp, fire captain of Station No. 1, said the blaze at Peabody Roady, which burned out of control for an hour before it was contained, probably was started by a trassh fire. The blaze endangered some nearby farm-land and the barn on it, but was extinguished before anything but grass was nurned.

Schuster said fires like the one on Peabody Road had been starting all day, especially in the northern part of the city and coutny. Schuster said some of the fires could have been the work of a arsonist, but careless burning was a more likely cause.

"We don't have any evidence there is an arsonist," Schuster said. "We sure hope we don't have someone running around starting fires on purpose, but there is that possibility."

APPENDIX 3
Exercises for Grammar and Punctuation

Punctuation Exercises (I)

Correct any punctuation errors in the following sentences.

1. The account executive, who was wearing a blue suit, was a Harvard graduate.

2. His wife Denise was in her 40s, but she acted like a 10 year old.

3. Her secretary Helen and her executive assistant, Bob, accompanied her.

4. The third office which has green drapes is Tom's.

5. The short stocky muscular young man was no member of the middle class.

6. The broken old man drank all alone in the smelly pink bar.

7. If employees care enough they will give an all out effort.

8. Nodding to him to come she smiled congenially.

9. The tall newly-constructed building is unsafe.

10. Because she knew the company well she trusted its products.

11. The age old truism took a strange new twist.

12. The friendly looking dog did not bother anyone.

13. The weak unsteady desk was poorly-constructed.

14. The computer which had just been repaired was destroyed in a fire.

15. The limousine had turned left and he could no longer see it.

16. He was old fashioned but he was not closed minded.

17. The tall brick house stood in a neatly-kept lot.

18. He never liked being interviewed, and often refused to see reporters.

19. Playing the game well, was important to her.

20. At the time of the murder she was out of town.

Punctuation Exercises (II)

Correct any punctuation errors in the following sentences.

1. The tall square building will be torn down.

2. The woman, who was eating the cherry pie, is a surgeon.

3. The thin balding middle-aged man is the president.

4. Because she was economy-minded she bought the small one.

5. His father was old fashioned but he loved video games.

6. He left his middle class neighborhood but he lost none of his middle class values.

7. The properly-trained secretary knew about non-restrictive clauses.

8. The company which had the better benefit package was her obvious choice.

9. The expensive blue tie appealed to the dapper young executive.

10. The canary yellow hat did not go with the heavy blue coat.

11. Before she worked here she worked there.

12. He tried hard yet he seldom succeeded.

13. She knew he would go, it was just a matter of time.

14. If I come I will not wear a tie.

15. What I need, is a long vacation.

16. Work proceeded nicely; and no one seemed to notice.

17. I was in charge and I accept full responsibility.

18. She succeeded, because she was immensely capable.

19. William did little work but he always seemed busy.

20. No one on the magazine staff agreed, therefore, the plan failed.

Pronoun Exercises

Correct any pronoun errors in the following sentences.

1. He took Tim and I to the movie.

2. Between you and I, pronouns can be difficult to use correctly.

3. He was the young man that caught the foul ball.

4. He did not know who to ask.

5. A writer must always check their sources.

6. The professor spoke to Jill and I just last week.

7. Whom do you think cheated on the exam?

8. People that work at home are happier than those who don't.

9. Instead of he and I, he chose she and Sheri.

10. The corporation guaranteed all of their products.

11. Everybody wishes they could write well.

12. It is me who should take the blame.

13. It was not whom you think it was.

14. Each student brought their own lunch.

15. The group is having their meeting this morning.

16. An architect should never publicize his fees.

17. She walked right behind Bill and I.

18. Who are you talking about?

19. A criminal must pay for their crime.

20. Is that her coming down the hall?

Exercises with Verbs and Verbals

Correct any errors in verb form in the following sentences.

1. If I was you, I wouldn't go.

2. The motion on the floor, if passed, will stop debate.

3. If more information is desired by you, please call.

4. He suddenly left the room, saying he was tired of questions.

5. Playing baseball in the park, his left leg was injured.

6. He only did that one time to thoroughly confuse the judges.

7. I will go there next week if the weather permits.

8. Maurice and all his friends likes hot dogs.

9. If that was the case, he would still be in office.

10. Working through the night, his back began to ache.

11. He only will have worked at the magazine for six months in February.

12. To be successful, good work habits are necessary.

13. If I was there, I surely would remember.

14. Bill, along with all of his buddies, love to dance.

15. The proposed constitutional amendment will ban same-sex marriage.

16. You will not ever do that again if I have anything to say about it.

17. Mary and those who think as she does is often wrong.

18. He hurried down the hall, saying he was late.

19. If he was really drunk, he would not be speaking so clearly.

20. He only did these exercises because he was asked to do them.

Springfield City Map

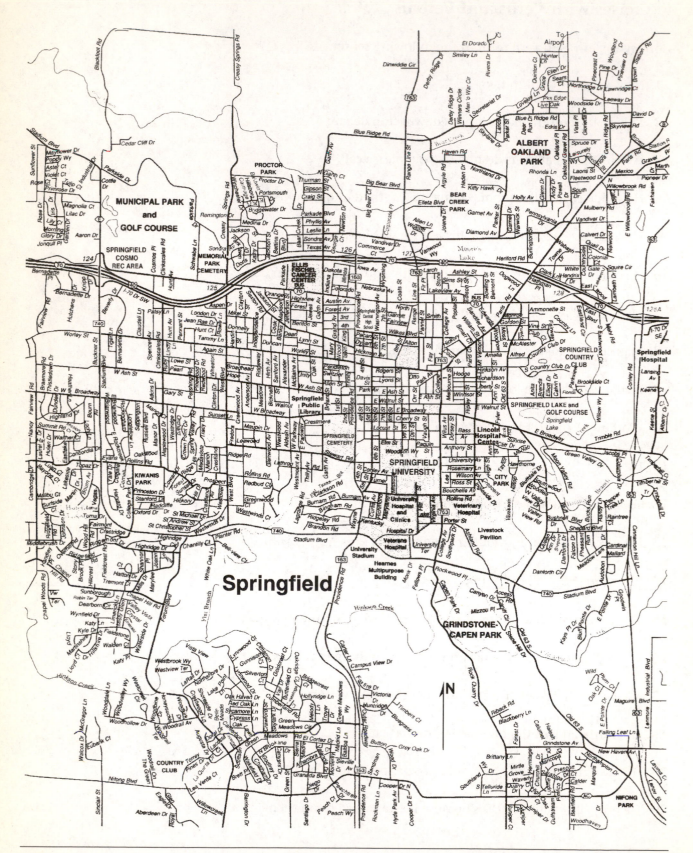

Springfield Directory of Institutions

Springfield City Government

Mayor: Juanita Williams
Police Chief: Paul Blakemore
City Clerk: Mary Cutts
Director of Water and Light Dept.: Megan Dinwiddie
First Ward: Hong Xiang
Second Ward: Juan Guttierez
Third Ward: Elizabeth R. Levine
Fourth Ward: Sherwin Imlay
Fifth Ward: Jun Ping Yang
Sixth Ward: Afua Noyes

Director of Community Services: Diane Acton
City Prosecutor: Louanne Barnes
City Treasurer: Loren Jungermann
City Auditor: Joseph Knight
Director of Public Works Dept.: Margaret Longfellow
City Manager: Diane Lusby
Director of City Finance Dept.: Thomas Nowell
Fire Chief: Bernard Perry
Fire Marshal: Capt. Anne Gonzalez
Director of Health Dept.: Ken Yasuda

Springfield Public School System

Superintendent: Max Schmidt
School Board President: Jerry Crawford

School Board Members: Janet Biss, James K. Lattimer, Rachel Pullman, Brian Schmidt, Anna Theiss

Springfield University

Chancellor: Bernadette Anderson
Director, University Library: Earl Burchfield
Vice Chancellor for Student Affairs: Brenda Daye
Dean, School of Medicine: Donald Faust
Dean, College of Business and Public Administration: Sherri Fitts
Dean, School of Law: Wu-Feng Fun
Dean, Graduate School: Harvey Gorjanc
Dean, College of Agriculture, Food and Natural Resources: George Huisman Jr.
Dean, Arts and Science: Luce Iragaray
Dean, College of Education: Kelle Juzkiw
Provost: Ronald Kemper
Assistant to the Chancellor for University Affairs: Jen-Lu Liao

Registrar and Admissions Director: Paul R. Meadows
Vice Chancellor for Development: Amanda Netdem
President: Michael R. Quinn
Dean, College of Engineering: Haroon Qureshi
Dean, School of Accountancy: LeRoy N. Rice
Dean, School of Journalism: John Seina
Vice Chancellor for Administrative Services: Jacob Singleton
Dean, School of Library and Informational Science: Dolores Von Flatern
Academic Affairs Vice President: Washington Wade
Dean, School of Human Environmental Sciences: Wen Wui Xu
Dean, College of Business and Public Administration: Min Hui Zhang

Lincoln County Government

Sheriff: Sue Fuller
Circuit Court Division I: Judge Robert Wagner
Circuit Court Division II: Judge Todd B. Schwartz
Circuit Court Division III: Judge Linda Garrett
Recorder of Deeds: Pauline Heinbaugh
County Assessor: Maria L. Kincaid

County Commission Members: Andrew Kramer, Joseph Reed, Nicole Ziden
County Clerk: Emily Parks
County Collector: Betty L. Ramsey
County Fire Protection District Chief: Debra A. Schuster
County Prosecuting Attorney: James Taylor

Springfield Hospital

Administrator: Rochelle Crowell
Chief of Staff: Kelly G. Maddox

Director of Public Information: Jose Tray

Springfield City Directory

A

Abbot, James (clerk, J.C. Penney Department Store), 2011 Garnett Drive

Abbott, Quentin (manager, Airport Administration), 1612 Limerick Lane, Apt. 4G

Abraham, Jesse (pilot, Springfield Regional Airport), 106 Highland Drive

Action, Larry D. (Spanish teacher), 1S E. Leslie Lane

Acton, Diane (director, Community Services), 407 Pecan St.

Adamms, Williams (secretary, Shelter Insurance), 1410 Forum Blvd.

Adams, Bill (director, Springfield Truck Inspections), 101 Sondra Ave.

Adams, Craig and Susan, 304 Texas Ave.

Adams, Jackson and Mary (accountant), 356 Pear Tree Circle; sons, Edward, Michael and James

Alger, Donn, 1607 Stonybrook Place

American Red Cross, 1805 W. Worley St.

Anderson, Bernadette (chancellor, Springfield University), 1532 Amelia St.

Anderson, John (retired) and Ruth, 88 Jefferson Drive

Applegate, Therese, 800 Sycamore Lane

B

Bach, John (accountant) and Raycene (attorney), 1698 N. Ann St.; daughters, Jacqueline and Jennifer

Baker, David (safety specialist, Springfield University Extension Service), 206 Oaklawn Drive

Bangle, Mike (heating technician), 1402 Rollins Road

Barnes, Harvey (architect), 1814 Oakcliff Drive

Barnes, Louanne (Springfield city prosecutor), 2000 Deerborne Circle

Barnridge, Mary (professor, Springfield University), 1456 Rosemary St.

Bartles, May (head librarian of Springfield), 3805 Barrington Drive

Baumer, Brad (owner, Brad's Books), 56 Hyde Park Drive

Betz, James (director, Parks and Recreation Dept.), 1804 Quarry Park Drive

Bhandary, Asha, 56 Treeland Road

Bietz, Jacob, 2600 Hikel St.

Biss, Janet (school board member), 4387 W. Broadway Ave.

Black Funeral Home, 2222 E. Broadway Ave.

Blackmore, Paul (retired), 1416 Shannon Place

Blackwater, Samuel (Parks and Recreation Dept.), 205 University Ave.

Blake, Bradford (sales rep., ABC Laboratories), 2304B Keane Drive

Blakemore, Paul (chief of police), 1705 Rebel Drive

Bliss, Janet (Columbia police officer), 2300 Hollyhock Drive

Bombauer, Maxine (social worker), 2009 Bridgewater Drive

Bowen, Lawrence K. (insurance salesman), 208 Maple Lane

Brock, K.L., 400 S. Sixth St.

Brock, Sharon, 700 Park de Ville Place

Brown, Rob (Lincoln County Fire Protection District), 240 Paris Road

Bucci, Dan (assistant general manager, Lincoln Downs Race Track), 4675 Worley St.

Burchard, Robert (basketball coach, Springfield College), 601 N. Ninth St.

Burchfield, Earl (director, Springfield University Library), 106 Business Loop 70 W.

Butler, Alfredo (laborer) and Lilah (salesclerk), 206 Elm St.

C

Chaney, May, 1600 Sylvan Lane

Channey, Bob (professor, chemical engineering), 3605 Madera Drive

Channey, Margaret, 812 Maplewood Drive

Chinn, Kahi, 303 Stewart St.

Chinn, Tom, 4201 Creasey Springs Road

Cipola, Christine, 1130 Ashland Road

Clark, Eric, 2500 Ridefield Road

Clark, Ethel, 200 Unity Drive

Clay, Wayne, Route 1

Cohen, Floyd, 507 Bourn Road

Cohen, Randy (student), 1516 Rosemary St.

Cohn, Randell (store manager, Express Lane), 204 Sexton Road E.

Conners, John (professor, engineering), 1300 University Ave.

Cornell, Pearl (volunteer, Springfield Hospital), Route 4

Cottey, Kim (sales associate, Walmart), 1603 Smiley Place

Craig, Duane (cook, Candle Light Lodge), 6206 Ridge Road

Craig, Vera (custodian), 3704 Danvers Drive

Crawford, Jerry (school board president), 2802 Butterfield Court

Crews, Roger, 2206 High Oak Court

Crookstein, Don and Jane (independent farmers), 1719 Highridge Circle; daughter, Jeanelle (student); son, Thom (student)

Crowell, Rochelle (administrator, Springfield Hospital), 212 Calvin Drive

Cruise, Roger (executive director, State Press Association), 2921 Oakland Road

Cunning, James W. (assistant manager, Hardee's), 505 W. Stewart Road

Cutts, Mary (city clerk), 1608 Princeton Drive

D

Daugherty, James (Springfield Fire Dept.), 1005 E. Broadway Ave.

Davis, Chris (self-employed oenologist), 1601 Smiley Place

Day, David (receptionist), 700 Hilltop Drive

Daye, Brenda (vice chancellor for student affairs, Springfield University), 5414 Boxwood Court

Dinwiddie, Megan (director, Water and Light Dept.), 1432 Garth Ave.

Douglas, Harold, 122 McBaine Ave.

Douglass, Thomas, 1521 Windsor St.

Drummond, Monica, 4527 W. Fourth St.

Du Bois, David, 1500 Forum Blvd.

Dubovick, John, 300 Providence Road

Dudley, Dennis, 320 Bridgewater Drive

Dunbar, Ralph, 706 Demaret Drive

Dyer, Julie, 20 Beverly Lane

E

Eifler, Jay, 200 Waugh St.

Eimer, William, 120 Paquin St.

Einfeld, Wendell, 111 S. Barr St.

Ennis, Tammy (student), 603 Juniper Ridge

Esposito, Nancy (staff nurse), 206 Ridgeway Ave.

Evenson, Gary (attorney, Evenson Ltd.), 3698 Chapel Hill Road

Evenson, Mary (computer operator, Dept. of Natural Resources), 511 High St.

Everson, Ala R. (janitor), 1704 Country Side Lane

F

Faith Baptist Church, 3711 Summit Road

Faust, Donald (dean, School of Medicine), 2909 Falling Leaf Lane

Fernandez, Carlos (media coordinator, Lincoln County), 3675 Sycamore Lane

Finney, Michael (priest, Newman Center), 3703 Lumpine Drive

First Baptist Church, 900 W. Broadway Ave.

Fitts, Sherri (dean, College of Business and Public Administration), 1318 St. Andrew St.

Fletcher, George, 321 Hickam Drive

Flint, Ernest, 500 Woodridge Drive

Flohra, Lee, 456 Oak Lawn Drive

Fuller, Sue (sheriff, Lincoln County), 709 Fairview Ave.

Fun, Wu-Feng (dean, School of Law), 1027 E. Broadway Ave.

G

Garrett, Linda (Lincoln County Circuit Court judge, Div. III), 2216 Concordia Drive

Glen, John (construction worker, Pike Construction), 508 Hunt Ave.

Gonzalez, Anne (Springfield fire marshal), 4645 Lynnwood Drive

Gorjanc, Harvey (dean, Graduate School, Springfield University), 811 Southampton Drive

Gorman, Steven (lieutenant, Fire Dept.), 2039 E. Walnut St.

Graham, Thomas C. (archaeologist), 1204 Manor Drive

Green, Ralph (pastor, Newman Center), 100 W. Worley St.

Gross Co. Engineers, 260 W. Broadway Ave.

Guttierez, Juan (Second Ward, City Council member) 3724 Southridge Drive

Guyton, John, 645 Haven Road

Guzy, Tina, 907 Kathy Drive

H

Harm, Erin, 20 Hourigan Circle

Harm, Sally (dietitian, Springfield Hospital), 2106 Chapel Hill Road

Harvey, A.G., 1400 Rosemary Lane

Harvey, Leta, 404 West Blvd. N.

Hassinger, Edward, 324 Mayflower Drive

Heaster, Shirley (beautician, Feminique Hair Salon), 1804 Grindley Ave.

Heinbaugh, Pauline (recorder of deeds), 16 Hitt St.

Henri, Margaret (telephone operator, AT&T), 3107a Hyde Park Drive

Henry, Thomas (physician), 222 South Jefferson St.

Higgins, Henry and Cloris (Realtor, West & Haver), 209 Fourth St.

Higins, Henry (waiter, Murry's), 3107 Green Meadows Way #4I

Hill-Young, Jennifer (botanist), 1995 Luna Lane

Hinckley, Thomas M. (program coordinator), 6 Edgewood St.

Hockman, Carl (operations analyst), 901 E. Cooper Drive

Hope, Raymond Lee (salesman, Springfield Auto Supply) and Mary, 1060 College Ave.

Huisman, George, Jr. (dean, College of Agriculture, Food and Natural Resources), 2009 Rose Drive

I

Iddings, Garrett, 444 Lenoir St.

Ide, Tony, 890 Bourne Ave.

Idel, Renee, 90 Keene St.

Imlay, Sherwin (Fourth Ward, City Council member), 2304 Mission Court

Iragaray, Luce (dean, School of Arts and Science), 1416 University Ave.

Ives, Paula R. (nurse, Springfield Hospital), 9951 E. Blvd.

Ivy, Patrick, 566 S. Ponderosa St.

Izmerian, Eleece, 764 Kittyhawk Drive

J

Jarvis, Angie, 906 E. Pointe Drive

Jashnani, Wendy, 324 Anthony St.

Jasperse, David, 9689 Blueridge Road

Joh__n, John (field service engineer), 406 Keene St.

Jo__n, Lindell B. (bus driver), 3033 Jellison St.

Jo__n, William R. (owner, Oakland Car Wash), 2120 __iley Lane

J____on, William S., 2505 Kyle Court

J__ John (Public Works Dept.), 2505 Kyle Court

J__ Ruth (marketing associate), 1501 Whitburn St.

J__rmann, Loren (city treasurer), 2236 Country Lane

J__w, Kelle (dean, College of Education), 1607 Park de __ville Place

K

__e, Ronald (publisher), 810 Again St.

__e, Angela (student), 263 Blue Ridge Road

__per, Ronald (provost, Springfield University), 425 __ Forum Blvd.

__stone, Charles (unemployed), 311 E. Ash St.

__caid, Maria L. (Lincoln County assessor), 2425 Colorado Ave.

__ight, Joseph (city auditor), 1314 Hinkson Ave.

__amer, Andrew (Lincoln County Commission member), 143 Glen Drive

__amer, Andrew A. (day care provider), 203 S. Ann St.

__onk, John (employee, Restwell Funeral Service), 2500 Waterside Drive

__ruger, Brent, 666 Lynnwood Drive

__ruse, Steve, 945 W. Broadway Ave.

__TGG-TV, 190 Business Loop 70 E.

__ueffer, Christine, 544 W. Wilbert Lane

L

La Chance, Duane (Gross Co. Engineers), 206 E. Woodrail Ave.

Lache, Ronald C. (salesman), 110 Alhambra Ave.

Lache, Ronald H. (retired lt. col.), 104 Alhambra Drive

Lache, Thelma (retired), 104 Alhambra Drive

Lattimer, James K. (school board member), 3622 Pimlico Drive

Lea, Wendy (teaching assistant, Springfield University), 1315 University Ave.

Lee, Rusty E. (extension associate, Springfield University Extension Service), 2180 Redbud Lane

Lehr, Angie (student), 6605 Hillstop Lane

Levine, Elizabeth R. (Third Ward, City Council member), 270 Fallwood Court

Levitt, Jon (teacher) and Sandra (office manager), 210 Maple Lane; son, Brad (student)

Liao, Jen-Lu (assistant to the chancellor for university affairs, Springfield University), 13 Arapaho Circle

Longfellow, Margaret (director, Public Works Dept.), 606 Mikel St.

Lopez, Fernando (watchman, T&L Electronics), 209 E. Watson Place

Lusby, Diane (city manager), 67 Gipson St.

Lynch, Merlyn, 3220 Holly Ave.

M

Maddox, Kelly B. (dentist), 909 Ashland Road

Maddox, Kelly G. (chief of staff, Springfield Hospital), 1632 Granada Drive

Madsen, Orrin, 13 Ninth St.

Manning, Greg (clerk, Brad's Books), 6 Spring Valley Road

Markison, Louis M. (computer analyst), 1605 Telluride Lane

Matten, Jeanne (lawyer), 306 Overhill Road

Maxwel, Thomas A. (president, Teamsters Local 1248), 300 Westwood Ave.

Maxwell, Thomas R. (public housing manager), 4410 Alan Lane

McClure, Pam (secretary), 1014 Southpark St.

McCubbins, Eugene (pastor, Faith Baptist Church), 15 Pendleton St.

Meadows, Paul R. (registrar and admissions director, Springfield University), 34 Middlebush Drive, Apt. 56

Memorial Park Cemetery, 909 Baldwin Place

Merchants National Bank, 600 E. Broadway Ave.

Miller, Rahsetnu (associate public defender, Lincoln County), 2085 E. Walnut St.

Miller, William H. (plant manager), 1716 Bettina Drive

Moore, David (professor, Springfield University), 345 College Ave.

Moore, Mary, 808 Again St.

Mose, Betsey (owner, Hideaway Bar and Grill), 200 Route K

N

Neal, Donna L. (student), 34 Waysite Drive

Neil, Madsen (retired), 119 Bicknell St.

Netdem, Amanda (vice chancellor for development, Springfield University), 2465 Sunset Lane S.

Newell, R.J. (manager, ACME Cleaning), 1308 Paris Road

Newman Center, 317 Brenda Lane

Ngo, Hier, 4067 Sylvan Lane

Nguyen, Trong, 998 Vandiver Drive

Nichols, Barbara, 9887 Clark Lane

Nichols, Virginia (architect), 115 Lake St.

Nishada, Milo (student), 438 College Ave., Apt. B

Nowell, Thomas (director, City Finance Dept.), 980 Rhonda Lane

Noyes, Afua (Sixth Ward, City Council member), 765 Unity Drive

O

Oats, Donald (receptionist), 1808 Bear Creek Drive

Oats, Tanya (hygienist), 207 N. Providence Road

Oglesby, James R. (stress lab coordinator), 1908 Iris Drive

Oglesby, Richard J. (staff nurse, Springfield Hospital), 4201 Rock Quarry Road

Omokaye, Gan, 231 Holly Ave.

Oncken, Christian, 4550 Otto Court

O'Neal, Harold, 544 Rangeline Road

Oney, Patricia, 880 Paquin St.

Osgood, Heather, 338 N. Garth Ave.

Oswalk, Carol, 7988 W. Rollins Road

P

Parker, David, 110 Ripley St.

Parker Funeral Service, 606 Washington Ave.

Parks, Emily (Lincoln County clerk), 521 Yuma Drive

Perkins, John (salesman, Springfield Lumber), 2933 Parkway Drive

Perrin, Daniel (student), 333 Stadium Blvd.

Perry, Bernard (fire chief, Springfield Fire Dept.), 8325 Worley St.

Pitts, Chris (janitor, Springfield University), 312 Anderson Drive

Pitts, Robert (carpenter), 210 Anderson Drive

Pliske, Gena (relief worker, Red Cross), 214 S. Ninth St.

Popandreau, George (owner, T&L Electronics), 3785 E. Terrace Road

Poplar, Jim, 5642 N. 11th St.

Pourot, Antoinette (student), 208A August Terrace

Prado, Dominic (insurance agent), 311 E. Worley St.

Property and Casualty Co., 303 First Ave.

Pullman, Rachel (school board member), 956 Ash St.

Q

Qian, Li, 344 University Ave.

Quade, Jennifer (student), 444 Jesse Lane

Quinlan, Steve, 700 W. Broadway Ave.

Quinn, Michael C., 306 Rockingham Drive

Quinn, Michael R. (president, Springfield University), 1416 College Ave.

Quisenberry, Nadine (account manager, Shelter Insurance), 222 Hinkson Ave.

Qureshi, Haroon (dean, College of Engineering), 1001 University Ave.

R

Rachel, Jerome, 700 English Drive

Rackley, Daniel, 98 W. Phyllis Ave.

Rains, Henry (house painter), 106 W. Ridgely Road

Ramsey, Betty L. (Lincoln County collector), 543 Falling Leaf Lane

Reed, Joseph (Lincoln County Commission member), 2155 Honeysuckle Drive

Restwell Funeral Service, 307 N. Ninth St.

Rice, LeRoy N. (dean, School of Accountancy), 45 Mission Court

Rice, Nancy (electrician), 1741 Riveria Drive

Rock Haven High School, 2025 S. Providence Road

Rodriguez, Henry (clerk, Target Department Store), 364 Peabody Lane; son, Ryan (student)

Rodriguez, Jose (assistant city manager, City of Springfield), 3114 Orchard Lane

Roets, Gary (owner, Gary's Jumbo Shrimp), 6204 Ridge Road

Roets, Rebecca, 602 Rollins Court

Rosen, Henry (Gross Co. Engineers), 411 S. Williams St.

Rudloff, Travis (mechanic), 1000 Prestwick Drive

S

Sapp, Dennis (Lincoln County Fire Protection District), 6651 Nifong Blvd.

Scanlon, Brennan (teacher, driver's ..., 304 Oakridge Court

Scanlon, Jim (basketball coach, S...gfield Central High), 1810 Creasy Springs Road

Schelpp, Melvin (retired), 209 Route ...

Scherr, Randall J. (chef), 301 Shepard ...t

Schmidt, Amy (teller, Commerce Ban... ...01 W. Phyllis Ave.

Schmidt, Brian (school board member...) 67 Ridgeway Ave.

Schmidt, Darin (telephone operator), 2... ...t. Joseph St.

Schmidt, Max (superintendent, Spring... School District), 5789 El Cortez St.

Schmitt, Brian (word processing opera... 2103 Riney Lane

Schuster, Debra A. (chief, Lincoln Cou... Fire Protection District), 946 Arbor Drive

Schwartz, Todd B. (Lincoln County Circ... ...ourt judge, Div. II), 856 Colonial Court

Sears, Doris (office manager, Sears Cons...tion), 1805 Lovejoy Lane

Seina, John (dean, School of Journalism... '11 Fairway Drive

Shaver, Scott (director, Lincoln County Planning Department), 2067 Skylark Drive

Singleton, Jacob (vice chancellor for administrative services, Springfield University), 573 Hunt Court

Smith, Irene (director, Green Meadows Preschool), 4560 Nifong Blvd.

Smith, Irene (retired), 1401 Business Loop 70 W.

Smyth, Mary (teacher, Green Meadows Day Care), 3567 Green Meadows Road

Sosinski, Marcelle, 2990 W. Hanover St.

Spencer Metal Processing Co., 211 E. Grindstone Ave.

Spillman, Roger (driver, Central Dairy), 2010 Rhonda Lane

Springfield Auto Supply, 6400 S.W. I-70 Drive

Springfield Central High School, 1000 Business Loop 70 E.
Springfield City Hall, 406 E. Broadway Ave.
Springfield Feed Co., 38 W. Elm St.
Springfield Hospital, 1600 E. Broadway Ave.
Springfield Memorial Cemetery, 104 Woodrail Ave.
Springfield Municipal Power Plant, 1004 Business Loop 70 E.
Stanfield, Paul (teacher), 4025 Grace Ellen Drive
Stark, Colleen M. (student), 534 Grand Ave.
Stephenson, Enid (realty manager), 316 Rock Quarry Road
Stone, Albert (retired), 2935 Parkway Drive
Stone, Mary, 1900 Rose Drive
Stookey, Timothy (student), 309 Lake Lane

T

T&L Electronics, 4404 U.S. Highway 90
Taylor, James (Lincoln County prosecuting attorney), 644 Misty Glen
Theiss, Anna (school board member), 323 Ridgemont Court
Thurmond, Stan (Springfield police officer), 19 Lemmon Drive
Townsend, Marshall, 88 Broadway Village Drive
Toyoshima, Satoshi, 988 Bernadette Drive
Tracy, Tammy, 800 Ashland Road
Tray, Jose (director of public information, Springfield Hospital), 799 Tracy Drive
Truman Sports Complex, 8301 Stadium Blvd.
Turner, Linda (dentist), 106 W. Burnam Road
Tyler, Richard, 877 Edgewood Ave.
Tyrolder, 9993 Sylvan Lane

U

Ubl, Gerald, 9000 Oak Cliff Drive
U-Haul Moving Center, 788 Sexton Road
Ukoha, Oruada, 800 Demaret Drive
United Medical, 888 E. Ash St.
United Pentecostal Church, 888 Benton St.
Upham, Bonnie, 300 Alexander Ave.
Uplinger, Andrew, 800 Strawn Road
Upson, Carl, 55 Woodrail Ave.
U.S. Army Adviser, 700 W. Ash St.
Uthlaut, Adam, 4300 W. Broadway Ave.

V

Vaca, Carlos (Columbia firefighter), 24 Pinewood Drive
Vago, Tony, 479 Kentucky Blvd.
Vair, Terry, 4088 S. Bethel Road
Varjack, Paul (freelance writer), 356 Argyle Road
Veach, Dennis (deputy chief, Springfield Police Dept.), 213 Texas Ave.
VFW Post 290, 1999 Ashley St.
Von Flatern, Dolores (dean, School of Library and Informational Science), 887 Conley Ave.
Voss, Dan, 4889 Mimosa Court

Vought, John, 2209 Hulen Drive
Vroegindewey, Linda, 47 E. Stewart Ave.
Vucheitch, Ginny, 4007 Woodrail Ave.

W

Wade, Washington (academic affairs vice president, Springfield University), 333 Fairmont St.
Wagner, Robert (Lincoln County Circuit Court judge, Div. I), 634 Evans Road
Wapniarski, Christy (student), 567 S. Williams St.
Watring, Cindy (student), 123 Columbus Hall
Welch, Emmy (manager, Dillards Department Store), 327 Glenwood Ave. S.
West, James (Parks and Recreation Dept.), 205 Nifong Blvd.
Westenhaver, James and Martha (president, Merchants National Bank), 300 E. Clark Lane
White, Clarence B. (intern), 1909 Dartmouth St.
Williams, Juanita (city mayor), 8479 Miller Drive
Woolkamp, Lynn (detective, Lincoln County Sheriff's Dept.), 765 Lakeshore Lane

X

Xenakis, Paul, 955 Woodrail Ave.
Xiang, Hong (First Ward, City Council member), 2801 W. Rollins Road
Xu, Feng, 4888 Amelia St.
Xu, Wen Wui (dean, School of Human Environmental Sciences), 104 E. Stewart Road

Y

Yang, Jun Ping (Fifth Ward, City Council member), 3107 Green Meadows Road
Yasuda, Ken (Health Dept. director), 897 Sycamore Lane
York, Dale, 488 W. Brookside Lane
York, Kim, 59 E. Hoedown Drive
Yost, Takuya, 4400 Hominy Branch
Youngquist, Luke, 344 Maryland Ave.
Youngwirth, Joseph, 25 N. Ninth St.
Younis, Amani, 408 Hitt St.
Yund, Glenn, 499 Waugh St.

Z

Zablow, John, 855 Lyon St.
Zafft, Jeff, 488 E. Phyllis Ave.
Zhang, Min Hui (dean, College of Business and Public Administration), 9760 Dripping Springs Road
Zhong, William, 455 Rock Quarry Road
Zhu, Jingcai, 488 S. College Ave.
Ziden, Nicole (Lincoln County Commission member), 4222 Brewer Drive
Zwonitzer, Gary, 555 Laurel St.
Zyk, Harvey, 8222 Stadium Blvd.
Zyk, Pam (City Council member), 8947 Stadium Blvd.
Zylstra, Alexandria, 455 Hitt St.

Acknowledgments (continued from p. iv)

Associated Press Leads. "A Flagstaff, Ariz., man who is suing the city is now its mayor" (May 16, 2012); "At least eight people are dead and more than 60 injured" (September 13, 2008); "The chief prosecutor of the International Criminal Court says . . ." (September 12, 2008); "St. Louis alderwoman Kacie Starr Triplett has proposed that the city's Delmar Boulevard receive the honorary name of Barack Obama Boulevard" (December 6, 2008); "The deputy state treasurer will become a trial judge in south-central Missouri (December 6, 2008); "A husband and wife are accused of breaking into about 60 homes around rural eastern Missouri" (December 6, 2008); "Expo 2012 has opened in South Korea's coastal city of Yeosu for a three-month run" (May 12, 2012); "Firefighters have put out a fire under part of a Los Angeles train wreck" (September 13, 2008); "Two skinhead youths to be extradited in 3 slayings" (March 9, 1995); "Some abortion clinic doctors want more than handguns for protection; they're buying armored cars" (1995); "Investigators are looking at 30 unsolved murder cases for possible links to a serial killer" (2008); "The Treasury Department is considering restricting each American" (November 21, 1990); "Home building plummets" (November 21, 1990). Copyright © The Associated Press. Reprinted with permission. All rights reserved.

Jennifer C. Kerr. From "FTC: Skechers deceived consumers with shoe ads." *USA Today Online*, May 17, 2012. Copyright © The Associated Press. Reprinted with permission. All rights reserved.

Missouri Press Association. Press release, "First Public Screening of Documentary About History of Missouri Newspapers Set for December 11 in Columbia." Reprinted by permission of the Missouri Press Association.